All Through the Night

Prayers and readings
from dusk till dawn

Edited by
Michael Counsell

CANTERBURY
PRESS
Norwich

Selection and original material
© Michael Counsell 2000

First published 2000 by
The Canterbury Press Norwich
(a publishing imprint of Hymns Ancient and
Modern Limited, a registered charity)
St Mary's Works, St Mary's Plain,
Norwich, Norfolk, NR3 3BH

British Library Cataloguing in Publication Data

A catalogue record for this book is available
from the British Library

ISBN 1-85311-350-6

Photoset by Regent Typesetting
Printed and bound in Great Britain by Biddles Ltd,
Guildford and King's Lynn

Contents

Introduction

Even in countries where church attendance is in decline, surveys frequently find that as many as seventy per cent of the people believe in God and eighty per cent pray. For many, personal difficulty is often the first impetus for prayer, and trouble never looms larger than in the sleepless early hours. Many others, conscious of the good gifts that they enjoy, only find time to give thanks at the end of a busy day. God rejoices in our differences and loves each one of us for our uniqueness, but two things which most human beings have in common are that the only leisure that they have to pray is at night, and that when we are tired or anxious it is hard to find the right words to use in prayer. This anthology of prayers and readings is for use from dusk to dawn, before we go to sleep or when we wake in the night.

Jesus taught that prayer should be as natural as a child and a parent chatting together. Yet, having used antiquated telephone systems in many different countries, I know how hard it is to carry on a conversation when you cannot actually hear the responses to your questions. But if you know the character of the person you are talking to well enough, it is usually possible to work out how you would expect them to answer. So it is with God, if by reading the Bible we have come to understand that God is love, that he expects those who love him to treat others with the same love and consideration as he shows us, and that his nature is to forgive. To pray to a God such as that is a lifelong delight.

So the beginning of prayer is thoughtful reading of the Bible. There are plenty of scriptural quotations in this volume; many publishers issue series of Bible reading notes, or you can read steadily through the Bible, a few verses each night, preferably leaving out the genealogies in Genesis and Matthew which, although they have something to teach us, are hardly fruitful for detailed meditation! For meditation consists in structured and prayerful thinking about God, and most teachers recommend the use of a lively imagination to put ourselves into the middle of the scene being described, or in the position of the writers and first hearers of the scriptural words. We can easily imagine the sights, sounds, smells, tastes and feelings that we would have at the time.

Most people can find a few minutes last thing at night or in the early morning to do this, and if you are awake when others are asleep, it is much better to use the time as an opportunity to meditate rather than to worry about insomnia, which only makes it worse. Having thought about the passage, we shall want to reflect on it prayerfully. Some people use the acronym 'ACTS' to remind themselves of what prayer is: Adoration, Confession, Thanksgiving and Supplication. We can talk to our God in our own words, no matter how informally, but if the words will not come easily, the use of other people's prayers from this book can set us off on the right track, or can sum up a period of extempore prayer. They can also lead us into contemplation.

If meditation is the art of thinking about God, contemplation is the enjoyment of God's presence without thinking, having quietened down the distractions of the busy brain. Again, the night is an excellent time to practise this, especially during periods of wakefulness. First it may be necessary to relax the tension in the muscles of the body. Some find it helpful to think of each group of muscles one by one, tense it up and then deliberately relax it: clench the fists, screw up the neck and face muscles and so on, and then feel them going limp. Next comes the control of the breathing, consciously making long, slow, deep breaths until that has become an unconscious pattern. Maybe while we are doing this we shall fall asleep, but if so, there is no harm done, for God wants us to refresh our bodies with sleep, and we may contemplate him in our dreams.

But if we stay awake, we can calm the mind with repeated phrases from memory. Many of the verses from the psalms in this book can be used as arrow prayers or mantras – shot up quickly to heaven, or repeated over and over until the mind is still. Use of a rosary, or any string of beads or knotted cord, may help us to slip into a pattern of regular repetition of any short prayer. In many parts of the Church, repeating what is called the Jesus Prayer is used to help us into contemplation: beginning with the words, 'Lord Jesus Christ, Son of the living God, have mercy on me, a sinner,' said in time with our breathing, we may gradually simplify it until we breathe in on the single word 'Jesus', imagining his love flowing into the inmost parts of our being, and then breathe out the word 'mercy', thinking of his love flowing out from our praying heart onto the needy world.

If this book is used to find a couple of quotations which will lull you to sleep, or to lead you into a period of meditation or contemplation, then it will have fulfilled its aim of helping you, whether you sleep or lie awake, to pray all through the night.

Michael Counsell
Honor Oak, London
January 2000

About the Author

Michael Counsell is the compiler of a number of major prayer collections, notably *2000 Years of Prayer*, also available from the Canterbury Press, *Prayers for Sundays* and *More Prayers for Sundays*, published by HarperCollins. He is also the author of *Every Pilgrim's Guide to Oberammergau*, published by the Canterbury Press. He is a parish priest in Forest Hill, south London.

At Close of Day

Much as we might wish to 'pray without ceasing' all day long, there is usually too much happening during the daylight hours to do more than shoot up quick arrow prayers, such as:

O Lord, you know how busy I must be today.
If I forget you, please do not forget me.

Sir Jacob Astley

Prayer and Praise

At the end of the day's work, however, it is time to praise God for his greatness and his goodness to us by day and night.

I T is good to give thanks to the Lord,
  and to sing praises to your name, God most high;
to tell of your mercy in the morning,
  and your trustworthiness every night.

Psalm 92:1–2

C OME now, turn aside for a while from your daily employment, escape for a moment from the tumult of your thoughts. Put aside your weighty cares, let your burdensome distractions wait, free yourself a while for God and rest awhile in him. Enter the inner chamber of your soul, shut out everything except God and that which can help you in seeking him, and when you have shut the door, seek him. Now, my whole heart, say to God, 'I seek your face; Lord it is your face that I seek.'

Anselm

WHEN Jesus had sent the crowd away, he set off by himself into the hills to pray. When evening came he was there alone.

Matthew 14:23

ERE I sleep, for ev'ry favour
This day showed
By my God,
I will bless my Saviour.

O my Lord, what shall I render
To thy name,
Still the same,
Merciful and tender?

Thou hast ordered all my goings
In thy way,
Heard me pray,
Sanctified my doings.

Leave me not, but ever love me;
Let thy peace
Be my bliss,
Till thou hence remove me.

Thou my rock, my guard, my tower,
Safely keep,
While I sleep,
Me, with all thy power.

So, whene'er in death I slumber,
Let me rise
With the wise,
Counted in their number.

John Cennick

ETERNAL Spirit,
flow through our being and open our lips
that our mouths may proclaim your praise.
Let us worship the God of Love.
Alleluia. Alleluia.

Jim Cotter

LET us offer up our praise as a sacrifice to God
through Jesus, a harvest of praise to him from our
lips, remembering also to do good to others and share
what we have with them, for sacrifices like that give
pleasure to God.

Hebrews 13:15–16

O Lord,
by triumphing over the power of darkness
you have prepared our place in the New Jerusalem;
grant us,
who have today given thanks for your resurrection,
to praise you in that city of which you are the light;
where with the Father and the Holy Spirit
you are alive and reign, now and for ever. Amen.

William Bright

PRAISE the Lord, you who are his servants.
We praise your name, O Lord,
because of your great glory,
Lord, King, Father of the Christ.
We praise you O Christ,
we sing hymns to you, we bless you,
the spotless Lamb
who took sin away from the world.

Praise is your fitting portion,
the singing of hymns to you is your due, and your glory;
yours, God the Father,
through the Son and in the Spirit,
age after age. Amen.

The Apostolic Constitutions

Thanksgiving

*It is always good to look back over the day that is
past, and remember how many things there are to be
thankful for.*

WE offer our thanks to you, O God;
we keep our promises to you, Most High.

Adapted from Psalm 50:14

O God, the life of all who live,
the light of the faithful,
the strength of those who labour,
and the repose of the dead:
we thank you for the blessings of the day that is past,
and humbly ask your protection through the coming
    night.
Bring us in safety to the morning hours:
through him who died and rose again for us,
your Son our Saviour Jesus Christ. Amen.

*The Book of Common Prayer
of the Episcopal Church of the USA*

WHEN upon life's billows you are tempest tossed,
When you are discouraged, thinking all is lost,
Count your many blessings: name them one by one,
And it will surprise you what the Lord hath done.
Count your blessings: name them one by one,
Count your blessings: see what God has done;
Count your blessings: name them one by one,
And it will surprise you what the Lord hath done.

Are you ever burdened with a load of care?
Does the cross seem heavy you are called to bear?
Count your many blessings: every doubt will fly,
And you will be singing as the days go by.
Count your blessings: name them one by one,
Count your blessings: see what God has done;
Count your blessings: name them one by one,
And it will surprise you what the Lord hath done.

J. Oatman

O God, the King eternal, whose light divides the day
from the night and turns the shadow of death into
the morning: drive far from us all wrong desires, incline
our hearts to keep your law, and guide our feet into the
way of peace; that having done your will with cheerful-
ness during the day, we may, when night comes, rejoice to
give you thanks; through Jesus Christ our Lord. Amen.

William Reed Huntington and William Bright

HEAVENLY Father, receive our evening sacrifice
of praise, and confession, and prayer, we pray. We
thank you for all the known and unknown mercies of
another day, for all the blessings of this life, for all the
means of grace, for all the riches of your salvation, and for
the hope of glory, that blessed hope, the coming of our

Lord Jesus Christ and our gathering together to him. We are one day nearer to that day. Teach us to live every day as those whose citizenship is in heaven, and who are looking for a Saviour from heaven, the Lord Jesus Christ. Amen.

Handley Moule

SWEET is the work, my God, my King,
 To praise thy name, give thanks and sing,
To show thy love by morning light,
And talk of all thy truth at night.

Isaac Watts

O Lord, heavenly Father, by whose divine ordinance the darkness covers the earth and brings unto us bodily rest and quietness, we render thee our hearty thanks for the loving-kindness which thou hast shown, in preserving us during the past day, and in giving us all things necessary for our health and comfort. And we beseech thee, for Jesus Christ's sake, to forgive us all the sins we have committed in thought, word, or deed, and that thou wilt shadow us this night under the wings of thy almighty power, and defend us from all power of the evil one. May our souls, whether sleeping or waking, wait upon thee, delight in thee, and evermore praise thee, so that when the light of day returns, we may rise with pure and thankful hearts, casting away the works of darkness and putting on the armour of light; through Jesus Christ. Amen.

Thomas Becon

I reverently speak in the presence of the Great Parent
   God:
I thank you that you have enabled me
to live this day, the whole day,
in obedience to the excellent spirit of your ways.

Shinto prayer, Japan

BLESSED are you,
   O Lord, the God of our fathers,
creator of the changes of day and night,
giving rest to the weary,
renewing the strength of those who are spent,
bestowing upon us occasions of song in the evening.
As you have protected us in the day that is past,
so be with us in the coming night;
keep us from every sin,
every evil and every fear;
for you are our light and salvation,
and the strength of our life.
To you be glory for endless ages. Amen.

Lancelot Andrewes

OUR help is in the name of the eternal God,
   who is making the heavens and the earth.

Dear God, thank you for all that is good,
for our creation and our humanity,
for the stewardship you have given us of this planet earth,
for the gifts of life and of one another,
for your love which is unbounded and eternal.

Jim Cotter

D A Y is dying in the west,
   Heav'n is touching earth with rest,
Wait and worship while the night
Sets her evening lamps alight
Through all the sky.
Holy, Holy, Holy, Lord God of Hosts!
Heav'n and earth are full of thee;
Heav'n and earth are praising thee, O Lord, most high.

Lord of life, beneath the dome
Of the universe, thy home,
Gather us, who seek thy face,
To the fold of thy embrace,
For thou art nigh.
Holy, Holy, Holy, Lord God of Hosts!
Heav'n and earth are full of thee;
Heav'n and earth are praising thee, O Lord, most high.

While the deep'ning shadows fall,
Heart of love enfolding all,
Through the glory and the grace
Of the stars that veil thy face,
Our hearts ascend.
Holy, Holy, Holy, Lord God of Hosts!
Heav'n and earth are full of thee;
Heav'n and earth are praising thee, O Lord, most high.

When for ever from our sight
Pass the stars, the day, the night,
Lord of angels, on our eyes
Let eternal morning rise,
And shadows end.
Holy, Holy, Holy, Lord God of Hosts!
Heav'n and earth are full of thee;
Heav'n and earth are praising thee, O Lord, most high.

Mary Artemisia Lathbury

After worship

On certain days, however, when part of the day has been busy with worship, the evening is a time for more unhurried reflection.

HOW lovely are your dwellings, Lord of hosts.
My heart is faint with longing for your courts;
my heart and my flesh cry out for the living God.
Even the sparrow has found a home,
and the swallow a nest where she may raise her chicks
in your sanctuary, Lord of hosts.
How happy are those who spend their lives in your house:
they will be always praising you!

Psalm 84:1–4

COME, thank the Lord, all you who serve the Lord,
who stand in the house of the Lord at night;
Lift up your hands in the sanctuary, and thank the Lord.
May the Lord bless you from Zion;
the maker of heaven and earth.

Psalm 134

GRANT, almighty God,
that the words
which we have heard this day with our outward ears,
may through your grace be so grafted inwardly in our
    hearts,
that they may bring forth in us the fruit of good living,
to the honour and praise of your name;
through Jesus Christ our Lord. Amen.

The Liturgy of St James

OUR day of praise is done;
  The evening shadows fall;
But pass not from us with the sun,
True Light that lightenest all.

Around the throne on high,
Where night can never be,
The white-robed harpers of the sky
Bring ceaseless hymns to thee.

Too faint our anthems here;
Too soon of praise we tire:
But O the strains how full and clear
Of that eternal choir!

Yet, Lord, to thy dear will
If thou attune the heart,
We in thine angels' music still
May bear our lower part.

'Tis thine each soul to calm,
Each wayward thought reclaim,
And make our life a daily psalm
Of glory to thy name.

A little while, and then
Shall come the glorious end;
And songs of angels and of men
In perfect praise shall blend.

John Ellerton

GRANT, O Lord,
that what we have said with our lips,
we may believe in our hearts
and practise in our lives;
and of your mercy keep us faithful to the end;
for Christ's sake. Amen.

John Hunter

Hospitality

When we return to our homes, the evening is a time for hospitality.

DO not forget to be hospitable. In this way some people have welcomed angels without realising it.

Hebrews 13:2

WHETHER the sun is riding high,
or moon and stars light up the sky,
the door is open to my hut.
Its catch will yield to all who try,
lest Christ himself should find it shut.
Whether my guest dwells in a hall,
or in a humble cattle-stall,
their hunger will I gladly feed.
What I have, I share with all,
lest Mary's Son should be in need.

Celtic

AS the two disciples approached the village they were heading for, Jesus seemed as though he was intending to go further. 'Please stay with us,' they begged him;

'It's almost evening and the sun is setting.' So he entered the house where they were staying. When they were at table, he took the bread, gave thanks to God, broke it and gave it to them. Suddenly they were able to recognise him.

Luke 24:28–31

FOR food, friends and fellowship, we thank you Lord through Jesus Christ. Amen.

Anonymous

SOME hae meat and canna eat,
and some wad eat that want it;
but we hae meat and we can eat,
and sae the Lord be thankit.

Robert Burns

Supplication

The evening may provide an opportunity to pray for ourselves (petition) and for others (intercession).

LORD, I cry to you, come to me quickly,
listen to my voice when I call you.
May my prayer be prepared like incense before you:
let the lifting of my hands be an evening sacrifice.

Psalm 141:1–2

JESUS told his disciples a parable, teaching them to keep praying and never give up. 'There was once a judge,' he said, 'who had no respect for God or anyone else. There was a widow in the same town who came to the judge. "Give me justice against my enemy," she demanded. For a while he refused, but then he sighed: "Even though I don't respect God or anyone else, I'll give this widow what she asks for. She's such a nuisance, she'll wear me out eventually!"' Then Jesus asked them, 'Do you hear what that wicked judge says? If even he gives justice at last, don't you think that God will patiently give justice to you whom he has chosen, when you cry out to him day and night? I tell you, God will do so very quickly.'

Luke 18:1–8

IN the evening Abraham called upon you on the mountain top and you answered him, O lover of us all; and in the evening we call upon you: come to our aid, O God, full of mercy, alleluia, and have mercy upon us, through Jesus Christ our Lord. Amen.

Syrian Orthodox

The Lord's Prayer: A New Unfolding

ETERNAL Spirit,
Life-Giver, Pain-Bearer, Love-Maker,
Source of all that is and that shall be,
Father and Mother of us all,
Loving God, in whom is heaven:

The Hallowing of your Name
echo through the universe!
The Way of your Justice
be followed by the peoples of the world!
Your Heavenly Will
be done by all created beings!
Your Commonwealth of Peace and Freedom
sustain our hope and come on earth!

With the bread we need for today,
feed us.
In the hurts we absorb from one another,
forgive us.
In times of temptation and test,
strengthen us.
From trials too great to endure,
spare us.
From the grip of all that is evil,
free us.

For you reign in the glory
of the power that is love,
now and for ever. Amen.

Jim Cotter

I am the source of your prayers, says Jesus: in the first place, I want you to receive a blessing; next, I make you want it; and finally I make you ask for it. How, then, could you possibly not receive what you ask for?

Julian of Norwich

ALMIGHTY Father, in your divine mercy you cover the earth with the curtain of night, so that all the weary may rest. Grant to us, and to all people, rest in you this night. Let your grace, we pray, comfort and support all who will spend it in sorrow, in loneliness, affliction, or in fear. We commend into your hands ourselves with all who are dear to us. Strengthen and confirm your faithful people, arouse the careless, relieve the sick, give peace to the dying, so that your holy name may be glorified in Christ Jesus, your Son, our Lord. Amen.

H. Stobart

BE mindful, O Lord, of your people here before you, and of those who are absent through age, sickness or infirmity. Care for the infants, guide the young, support the aged, encourage the faint-hearted, collect the scattered, and bring back the wandering to your fold. Travel with the voyagers, defend the widows, shield the orphans, deliver the captives, heal the sick. Succour all who are in tribulation, necessity or distress. Remember for good all those who love us, and those who hate us, and those who have desired us, unworthy as we are, to pray for them. And those whom we have forgotten, Lord, remember. Grant unto each according to your merciful loving-kindness, and your eternal love; through Jesus Christ our Lord. Amen.

Orthodox

ALMIGHTY God, who hast given us grace at this time with one accord to make our common supplications unto thee; and hast promised that when two or three are gathered together in thy name thou will grant their requests: Fulfil now, O Lord, the desires and petitions of thy humble servants, as may be most expedient for them; granting us in this world knowledge of thy truth, and in the world to come, life everlasting. Amen.

Orthodox, in The Book of Common Prayer

Rest for the weary

At the end of the day's labour, God gives his children the opportunity to rest.

RETURN to your rest, my soul, for the Lord has blessed you.

Psalm 116:7

WHO will give me the wings of a dove, I cried,
  so that I could fly away and be at rest?
See how far away I would flee,
making my home in the wilderness.

Psalm 55:6–7

JEZEBEL sent a messenger to Elijah, to say, 'May God
  strike me dead if I do not end your life tomorrow.'
Elijah was afraid, and fled for his life, travelling for a
whole day into the wilderness. When night came he settled
down under a gorse bush. He prayed, begging God to kill
him. 'I've had enough, Lord; take my life, I'm no better
than my ancestors were.' As he lay asleep under the gorse
bush, an angel touched him and said, 'Get up, Elijah, and
eat something.' He woke up and saw near his head a cake
baked on hot stones, and a jar of water. So he ate and
drank, and lay down to sleep. Later the angel of the Lord
came to him a second time and touched him, saying, 'Get
up and eat, or the journey will be too much for you.' So he
got up, ate and drank, and that food gave him enough
strength to travel for forty days and forty nights to Horeb,
the Mountain of God.

1 Kings 19:2–8

A sabbath rest still remains for the people of God;
  for those who enter God's rest cease from their
     labours
in the same way as God did from his.

Hebrews 4:9–10

O Quanta Qualia Sunt Illa Sabbata

O what their joy and their glory must be,
  Those endless Sabbaths the blessed ones see!
Crown for the valiant; to weary ones rest;
God shall be all, and in all ever blest. . . .

We, where no trouble distraction can bring,
Safely the anthems of Sion shall sing;
While for thy grace, Lord, their voices of praise
Thy blessed people shall evermore raise. . . .

Low before him with our praises we fall,
Of whom, and in whom, and through whom are all;
Of whom, the Father; and through whom, the Son;
In whom, the Spirit, with them ever one. Amen.

Peter Abelard

THUS says the Lord God, the Holy One of Israel: In
  returning and rest you will be saved; in quietness and
in trust your strength shall be.

Isaiah 30:15

JESUS said: 'Come here to me, all you who are weary
  and are carrying heavy loads, and I will give you rest.
Take my yoke upon you, and learn from me; for I am
gentle, my heart is humble, and you will find rest for your
souls. For my yoke is easy, and my burden is light.'

Matthew 11:28

THE Lord is my pace-setter, I shall not rush,
  He makes me stop and rest for quiet intervals,
He provides me with images of stillness,
  which restore my serenity.
He leads me in the ways of efficiency,

through calmness of mind,
And his guidance is peace.
Even though I have a great many things
   to accomplish each day,
I will not fret for his presence is here.
His timelessness, his all-importance
   will keep me in balance.
He prepares refreshment and renewal
   in the midst of my activity
By anointing my mind with his oils of tranquillity,
My cup of joyous energy overflows.
Surely harmony and effectiveness
   shall be the fruits of my hours,
For I shall walk in the pace of my Lord,
   and dwell in his house for ever.

Toki Miyashina

AND now the wants are told, that brought
   Thy children to thy knee;
Here lingering still, we ask for nought,
But simply worship thee.

The hope of heaven's eternal days
Absorbs not all the heart
That gives thee glory, love, and praise,
For being what thou art.

For thou art God, the One, the Same,
O'er all things high and bright;
And round us, when we speak thy name,
There spreads a heaven of light.

O wondrous peace, in thought to dwell
On excellence divine;
To know that nought in us can tell
How fair thy beauties shine!

O thou, above all blessing blest,
O'er thanks exalted far,
Thy very greatness is a rest
To weaklings as we are;

For when we feel the praise of thee
A task beyond our powers,
We say, 'A perfect God is he,
And he is fully ours.'

All glory to the Father be,
All glory to the Son,
All glory, Holy Ghost, to thee,
While endless ages run.

William Bright

Evensong

BLEST be the God of love,
   Who gave me eyes, and light, and power this day,
Both to be busy, and to play.
But much more blest be God above,
Who gave me sight alone,
Which to himself he did deny:
For when he sees my ways, I die:
But I have got his Son, and he hath none.

What have I brought thee home
For this thy love? have I discharged the debt,
Which this day's favour did beget?
I ran; but all I brought, was foam,
Thy diet, care, and cost
Do end in bubbles, balls of wind;
Of wind to thee whom I have crost,
But balls of wild-fire to my troubled mind.

19

Yet still thou goest on,
And now with darkness closest weary eyes,
Saying to man, It doth suffice:
Henceforth repose; your work is done.
Thus in thy ebony box
Thou dost inclose us, till the day
Put our amendment in our way,
And give new wheels to our disorder'd clocks.

I muse, which shows more love,
The day or night; that is the gale, this the harbour;
That is the walk, and this the arbour;
Or that the garden, this the grove.
My God, thou art all love.
Not one poor minute 'scapes thy breast,
But brings a favour from above;
And in this love, more than in bed, I rest.

George Herbert

The Pulley

WHEN God at first made Man,
    Having a glass of blessings standing by,
'Let us' said he, 'pour on him all we can;
Let the world's riches, which dispersed lie,
Contract into a span.'

So strength first made a way;
Then beauty flowed, then wisdom, honour, pleasure:
When almost all was out, God made a stay,
Perceiving that, alone of all his treasure,
Rest in the bottom lay.

'For if I should,' said he,
'Bestow this jewel also on my creature,

He would adore my gifts instead of me,
And rest in Nature, not the God of Nature;
So both should losers be.

'Yet let him keep the rest,
But keep them with repining restlessness;
Let him be rich and weary, that at least,
If goodness lead him not, yet weariness
May toss him to my breast.'

George Herbert

On Going to Bed

ON the pillow of my bed
as I lay down my weary head;
as my body takes its rest,
in your mercy, Lord, I pray,
let me, at the close of day
rest my soul upon your breast.

Beneath the blankets warmth is formed;
may my soul by love be warmed;
as my mind is filled with dreams,
as I rest in slumber deep,
fill my soul, while still asleep,
with the light of heaven's gleams.

Johann Freylinghausen

LET us not seek outside you what we can find only in
you, O Lord: peace and rest, and joy and bliss, which
dwell in your abiding joy. Lift up our souls above the
weary round of harassing thoughts to your eternal presence. Lift up our souls to the pure, bright, serene, radiant
atmosphere of your presence, that there we may breathe
freely, there repose in your love, there be at rest from ourselves and from all things that weary us, and return with

the armour of your peace to endure whatever tasks you set us; for the sake of Christ Jesus our Lord. Amen.

Edward Pusey

O Lord our God, refresh us with quiet sleep when we are wearied with the day's labour, that, being assisted with the help which our weakness needs, we may be devoted to you both in body and mind, through Jesus Christ our Lord. Amen.

The Leonine Sacramentary

CREATOR and sustainer of all that is,
you make darkness and it is night,
and have made us to go out to our work
and to our labour until it is evening;
grant that having done our daily tasks through your grace
we may rest this night in your eternal love;
through Jesus Christ our Lord. Amen.

Michael Counsell

MERCIFUL Lord, of thy abundant goodness towards us thou hast made the day wherein to work, and ordained the night wherein to take our rest; grant us such rest of body, that we may have a waking soul. Let no vain and wandering fancy trouble us; let our spiritual enemies have no power over us, but let our minds be set wholly upon thy presence, to love, and fear, and rest in thee alone, that being refreshed with moderate and sober sleep, we may rise up again, with cheerful strength and gladness, to serve thee in all good works; through Jesus Christ our Lord. Amen.

John Cosin

J ESUS our brother, as you took your disciples aside when they were weary because there was so much coming and going, and called them to rest a while, look upon us when we are tired at the end of the day. Calm the storms in our troubled minds, forgive us the sins which trouble our consciences and the doubt and anger which cause our faith to waver. Teach us to trust God, and to trust you also, that we may sleep in peace, and awake refreshed for your service. We ask this because you are our Master and our Friend, Jesus Christ our Lord. Amen.

Michael Counsell

B E present, O merciful God,
and protect us through the silent hours of this night,
so that we who are wearied by the changes and chances
    of this fleeting world
may repose upon your eternal changelessness;
through Jesus Christ our Lord. Amen.

The Leonine Sacramentary

O God, by making the evening to succeed the day, you have bestowed the gift of repose on human weakness; grant, we pray, that while we enjoy those timely blessings we may acknowledge him from whom they come, Jesus Christ our Lord. Amen.

The Mozarabic Sacramentary

Celtic blessing prayers

The Celtic peoples who inhabited Britain before the Anglo-Saxon invasion, and who remained in Cornwall, Wales, Ireland and Scotland, had many prayers for use at close of day. Here is an assortment from those collected and translated in the Hebrides islands by Alexander Carmichael.

Sleeping Prayer

I am placing my soul and my body
  On Thy sanctuary this night, O God,
On Thy sanctuary, O Jesus Christ,
On Thy sanctuary, O Spirit of perfect truth,
    The Three who would defend my cause,
    Nor turn Their backs upon me.

Thou, Father, who art kind and just,
Thou, Son, who didst overcome death,
Thou, Holy Spirit of power,
Be keeping me this night from harm;
    The Three who would justify me
    Keeping me this night and always.

Carmina Gadelica I, 73

The Sleep Prayer

I am now going into the sleep,
  Be it that I in health shall waken;
If death be to me in the death-sleep,
Be it that on Thine own arm,
O God of Grace, I in peace shall waken;
    Be it on Thine own beloved arm,
    O God of Grace, that I in peace shall waken.

Be my soul on Thy right hand, O God,
Thou King of the heaven of heavens;
Thou it was who bought'st me with Thy blood,
Thou it was who gavest Thy life for me,
  Encompass Thou me this night, O God,
  That no harm, no evil shall me befall.

Whilst the body is dwelling in the sleep,
The soul is soaring in the shadow of heaven,
Be the red-white Michael meeting the soul,
Early and late, night and day,
  Early and late, night and day.

Amen.

Carmina Gadelica I, 85

Bed Blessing

I am lying down to-night as beseems
  In the fellowship of Christ, son of the Virgin of
    ringlets.
In the fellowship of the gracious Father of glory,
In the fellowship of the Spirit of powerful aid.

I am lying down to-night with God,
And God to-night will lie down with me,
I will not lie down to-night with sin, nor shall
Sin nor sin's shadow lie down with me.

I am lying down to-night with the Holy Spirit,
And the Holy Spirit this night will lie down with me,
I will lie down this night with the Three of my love,
And the Three of my love will lie down with me.

Carmina Gadelica I, 83

Sleep Consecration

I lie down tonight
With fair Mary and with her Son,
With pure-white Michael,
And with Bride beneath her mantle.

I lie down with God,
And God will lie down with me,
I will not lie down with Satan,
Nor shall Satan lie down with me.

O God of the poor,
Help me this night,
Omit me not entirely
From Thy treasure-house.

For the many wounds
That I inflicted on Thee,
I cannot this night
Enumerate them.

Thou King of the blood of truth,
Do not forget me in Thy dwelling-place,
Do not exact from me for my transgressions,
Do not omit me in Thine ingathering.
    In Thine ingathering.

Carmina Gadelica I, 81

Night Prayer

IN Thy name, O Jesu Who wast crucified,
    I lie down to rest;
Watch Thou me in sleep remote,
    Hold Thou me in Thy one hand;
        Watch Thou me in sleep remote,
            Hold Thou me in Thy one hand.

Bless me, O my Christ,
  Be Thou my shield protecting me,
Aid my steps in the pitful swamp,
  Lead Thou me to the life eternal;
    Aid my steps in the pitful swamp,
      Lead Thou me to the life eternal.

Keep Thou me in the presence of God,
  O good and gracious Son of the Virgin,
And fervently I pray Thy strong protection
  From my lying down at dusk to my rising at day;
    And fervently I pray Thy strong protection
      From my lying down at dusk to my rising at day.

Carmina Gadelica III, 329–31

Thou Great God

THOU great God, grant me Thy light,
  Thou great God, grant me Thy grace,
Thou great God, grant me Thy joy,
  And let me be made pure in the well of Thy health.

Lift Thou from me, O God, my anguish,
  Lift Thou from me, O God, my abhorrence,
Lift Thou from me, O God, all empty pride,
  And lighten my soul in the light of Thy love.

As I put off from me my raiment,
  Grant me to put off my struggling;
As the haze rises from off the crest of the mountains,
  Raise Thou my soul from the vapour of death.

Jesu Christ, O Son of Mary,
  Jesu Christ, O Paschal Son,
Shield my body in the shielding of Thy mantle,
  And make pure my soul in the purifying of Thy grace.

Carmina Gadelica III, 345

The Pilgrims' Safeguarding

I am placing my soul and my body
  Under thy guarding this night, O Brigit,
O calm Fostermother of the Christ without sin,
O calm Fostermother of the Christ of wounds.

I am placing my soul and my body
Under thy guarding this night, O Mary,
O tender Mother of the Christ of the poor,
O tender Mother of the Christ of tears.

I am placing my soul and my body
Under Thy guarding this night, O Christ,
O Thou Son of the tears, of the wounds, of the piercings,
May Thy cross this night be shielding me.

I am placing my soul and my body
Under Thy guarding this night, O God,
O Thou Father of help to the poor feeble pilgrims,
Protector of earth and of heaven,
    Protector of earth and of heaven.

Carmina Gadelica III, 321

Nightfall

Lighting the lamps

Basil the Great wrote: 'Our ancestors did not think it right to accept the blessing of lamplight in the evening in silence. The moment it appeared, they would thank God for it. Who the author of this hymn of thanksgiving was we cannot say, but it is very old and the people still sing it:'

HAIL, gladdening light, of his pure glory poured
Who is the immortal Father, heavenly, blest,
Holiest of Holies, Jesus Christ our Lord!
Now we are come to the sun's hour of rest,
The lights of evening shine,
We hymn the Father, Son, and Holy Spirit divine.
Worthiest art thou at all times to be sung
With undefilèd tongue,
Son of our God, giver of life, alone:
Therefore in all the world thy glories, Lord, they own.

Phos hilaron

GOD said, 'Let there be light,' and there was light. God saw that the light was good, and God separated the light from the darkness. God called the light 'Day' and the darkness 'Night'. There was evening, and there was morning: it was the first day.

Genesis 1:3–5

YOUR word is a lamp for my feet
and a light on my path.

Psalm 119:105

WE thank you, God, through your Child, Jesus
Christ our Lord, because you have enlightened us
and revealed to us the light which will never grow dim.
The day's allotted span is over; we have reached the
beginning of the night. You created the daylight for our
pleasure, and we have had our fill of it. Now evening has
come and the lamps are lit; again we have enough light to
see by, so we praise your holiness and glory, through your
only Son, our Lord Jesus Christ.

Hippolytus

ALMIGHTY God,
we give you thanks for surrounding us,
as daylight fades,
with the brightness of the vesper light;
and we implore you of your great mercy that,
as you enfold us with the radiance of this light,
so you would shine into our hearts
the brightness of your Holy Spirit;
through Jesus Christ our Lord. Amen.

Ambrosian Vespers

O Lord, give us, we pray, in the name of Jesus your
Son our Lord, that love which can never cease, that
will kindle our lamps but not extinguish them, that they
may burn in us and enlighten others. Christ, our dearest
Saviour, kindle our lamps, that they may evermore shine
in your Temple, that they may receive unquenchable light
from you that will enlighten our darkness, and lessen the
darkness of the world. Lord Jesus, we ask you to give your

light to our lamps, that in its light the most holy place may be revealed to us where you dwell as the eternal priest, that we may always behold your face, desire you, look on you in love, and long after you, for your own sake. Amen.

St Columba

GREAT God, dwelling in light invisible,
 creator of all things in your wisdom,
you divided the light from the darkness,
you set up the sun to govern the day,
the moon and the stars to rule the night.
You have allowed us sinners to live to this hour,
and to come into your presence with our evening praise.
Lover of us all,
let our prayers go up to you like the incense,
and accept them as an evening sacrifice.
Grant that this night may be spent in peace;
clothe us with the armour of light.
May we remember your presence through the darkness,
and rise in the morning in gladness of soul.
We lift our hearts in praise to you,
Father, Son and Holy Spirit,
now and always and for ever and ever. Amen.

Orthodox, prayer at lamp-lighting

GRANT me, O Lord, the lamp of love which never
 grows dim,
that it may shine in me and warm my heart,
and give light to others through my love for them,
and by its brightness we may have a vision of the Holy
 City
where the true and inextinguishable light shines,
Jesus Christ our Lord.

Columbanus

J ESUS said, 'Nobody lights a lamp in order to hide it under a basket! You stand it on a ledge, so that it can give light to everyone in the house.'

Matthew 5:15

J ESUS said, 'The kingdom of heaven is like the story of the ten bridesmaids with their oil-lamps, waiting to meet the bridegroom. Five were sensible and five were silly. The stupid ones did not take any spare oil for their lamps. But the clever ones each took a flask of oil. The bridegroom was late, so they all fell asleep. At midnight they were woken by somebody shouting "Look! The bridegroom is coming. Go out and meet him." All the bridesmaids tried to get their lamps ready. The silly ones were pleading with the sensible ones: "Please give us some of your oil," they begged. "Our lamps are going out!" "Certainly not," answered the sensible ones. "If we did, nobody would have enough! Go to the shop and buy some more oil." While they were away the bridegroom arrived, and the bridesmaids who were ready went into the wedding reception. The silly girls hurried back, calling out, "Sir, sir, open up and let us in!" But the bridegroom answered, "I'm sure I don't know who you are!"'

Matthew 25:1–12

E TERNAL God, thou hast warned us that thy Son the Bridegroom will come at midnight, at an hour when we are least aware. Let us ever hear the cry, 'The bridegroom is coming', so that we may never be unprepared to meet him, our Lord and Saviour Jesus Christ. Amen.

Lancelot Andrewes

BEHOLD, the Bridegroom comes in the middle of the night; and blessed is the servant whom he shall find watching, but unworthy is the one whom he shall find in slothfulness. Grant then, Lord, that we may not be overcome by the sleep of the soul, lest we be given over to death and shut out from the kingdom; have mercy on us through Jesus Christ our Lord. Amen.

Orthodox

The cross to guard us

As we turn to God for protection through the night, the cross is the symbol of his love, which is greater than any other power.

JESUS is the first of all, because the full divine nature is in him. Through Jesus, God reconciles everything to himself, making peace by means of the blood which he shed on the cross.

Colossians 1:19–20

THE sun is sinking fast,
   The daylight dies;
Let love awake, and pay
Her evening sacrifice.

As Christ upon the cross,
In death reclined,
Into his Father's hands
His parting soul resigned,

So now herself my soul
Would wholly give
Into his sacred charge,
In whom all spirits live;

So now beneath his eye
Would calmly rest,
Without a wish or thought
Abiding in the breast,

Save that his will be done,
Whate'er betide,
Dead to herself, and dead
In him to all beside.

Edward Caswall

LORD, let me rest the ladder of gratitude against your cross and, mounting, kiss your feet.

An Indian Christian

MAY the cross of the Son of God, who is mightier than all the powers of evil, abide with you in your going out and your coming in! From the wrath of evil people, from the temptations of the devil, from all low passions that beguile the soul and body, may it guard, protect and deliver you: and may the blessing of God almighty, the Father, the Son and the Holy Spirit, be among you and remain with you always.

An Indian Christian

O Lord Jesu Christ,
   Son of the living God,
we pray thee to set thy passion, cross and death
between thy judgement and our souls,
now and in the hour of our death.
Vouchsafe to grant mercy and grace to the living,
rest to the dead,
to thy holy Church peace and concord,
and to us sinners everlasting life and glory;

for thou art alive and reignest,
with the Father and the Holy Spirit,
one God for ever and ever. Amen.

Hours of the Blessed Virgin Mary

A S now the sun's declining rays
       At eventide descend,
E'en so our years are sinking down
    To their appointed end.

Lord, on the cross thine arms were stretched
    To draw the nations nigh;
O grant us then that cross to love,
    And in those arms to die.

To God the Father, God the Son,
    And God the Holy Ghost,
All glory be from saints on earth,
    And from the angel host.

Charles Coffin

O Lord Jesus Christ, son of the living God,
    who at this evening hour didst rest in the sepulchre,
and didst thereby sanctify the grave
    to be a bed of hope to thy people:
make us so to abound in sorrow for our sins,
which were the cause of thy passion,
that when our bodies lie in the dust,
our souls may live with thee;
who livest and reignest with the Father and the Holy
    Ghost,
one God, world without end. Amen.

Cuddesdon Office Book

God, protect our loved ones

We pray also for God to protect through the night all those whom we love.

YOU shall not fear the Terror by night,
  nor the arrow that flies by day;
the plague that stalks in the darkness,
nor the Destroyer who lays waste at noon.
God will put you in the care of his angels,
who will look after you wherever you go.

Psalm 91:5–6, 11

ACCEPT, we beseech thee, O Lord, our praises and supplications, and look graciously upon this household, that we may abide this night in peace and safety, under the shadow of thy wings, and so assist us by thy grace that we may be fitted for that kingdom where there shall be no more sin, nor sorrow, neither any more pain, but all shall be joy and peace in the Holy Ghost; to whom with thee, O Father, and thee, O blessed Jesus, be all glory, both now and evermore. Amen.

Edward Meyrick Goulburn

VISIT our homes, O Lord, we pray,
  and drive far from them all the snares of the enemy;
let your holy angels dwell therein to preserve us in peace;
and may your blessing be upon us evermore;
through Jesus Christ our Lord. Amen.

The Breviary

ETERNAL God, you watch over us all;
grant that the friendships formed between us here
may neither through sin be broken,
nor hereafter through worldly cares be forgotten;
but that bound together across the world
by the unseen chain of thy love,
we may be drawn nearer to you
and nearer to each other,
through Jesus Christ our Lord. Amen.

Balliol Boys' Club

WE commend to you, O Lord,
our souls and our bodies,
our minds and our thoughts,
our prayers and our hopes,
our health and our work,
our life and our death;
our parents and brothers and sisters,
our benefactors and friends,
our neighbours, our countrymen,
and all Christian folk this day and always.

Lancelot Andrewes

INTO your hands, Lord, we commit ourselves, our spirit, soul and body. You have created and you have redeemed them, Lord God of truth. And with ourselves, we commend all our friends, and all our possessions. You, Lord, have graciously given them to your servants. Preserve our down-sitting and our uprising, from this time forth and evermore. May we remember you as we lie on our bed, and when we wake, find you still with us. We will lie down in peace and sleep, for you, Lord, alone can make us dwell in safety. Hear us and answer us, we humbly pray; for the sake of Christ Jesus our Lord. Amen.

Lancelot Andrewes

I kneel in prayer before God,
the Father of our Lord Jesus Christ,
who has given a name and a purpose
to every family in heaven and on earth,
asking that he may give you,
out of his glorious wealth,
the power to become strong
through the indwelling of his Spirit,
Christ abiding in your heart
by means of your faith.
May you strike deep roots in the love of Christ,
able to grasp, with all God's people,
how wide and long and deep and high God's love is,
and know that love for yourselves,
even though it is too great
for anyone to know completely,
because you too are filled
with the divine nature.

Ephesians 3:14–19

BLESS, O Lord, this house and all who dwell in it, as you blessed the homes of Abraham, Isaac, and Jacob; that within these walls may dwell an angel of light, and that we who dwell together in it, may receive the abundant dew of heavenly blessing, and through your tenderness rejoice in peace and quiet; through Jesus Christ our Lord. Amen.

The Gelasian Sacramentary

INTO thy hands,
O Father and Lord,
we commend this night our souls and our bodies,
our parents and homes,
friends and colleagues,

neighbours and kindred,
our benefactors and the faithful departed,
all folk rightly believing,
and all who need thy pity and protection:
light us with thy holy grace,
and suffer us never to be separated from thee,
O Lord in Trinity, God everlasting. Amen.

Edmund Rich

O UR God, you open your hand,
  and fill all things living with plenteousness;
to you we commit all those who are dear to us;
watch over them, we pray,
and provide all things needful for their souls and bodies,
now and for evermore;
through Jesus Christ our Lord. Amen.

Nerses

In the evening of life

We think of those who are approaching the evening of their days, and we pray for ourselves as we grow older.

I was young, and now I am old,
  yet I have never seen good people abandoned by God,
nor their children begging for bread.

Psalm 37:25

N OW that I am old and grey-headed,
  Lord, do not leave me,
until I have told this new generation about your strength,
and the unborn children about your power.

Psalm 71:18

ABIDE with us, O Lord,
for it is toward evening and the day is far spent;
abide with us, and with your whole Church.
Abide with us in the evening of the day,
in the evening of life,
in the evening of the world.
Abide with us and with all your faithful ones,
O Lord, in time and in eternity. Amen.

Lutheran Manual of Prayer

GROW old along with me!
The best is yet to be,
The last of life, for which the first was made:
Our times are in his hand
Who said, 'A whole I planned,
Youth shows but half; trust God: see all, nor be afraid.'

Robert Browning

ONCE my hair was bright and blond, it fell in long
ringlets either side of my brow; now it is grey and
thin, its beauty is all gone. Once as I walked along the
road the girls would turn their heads to look at me; now
no woman looks my way, no heart beats faster as I pass
by. Once my body burned with desire, and I had the
strength to do what I wished; now desire has grown cold,
I have no energy to satisfy even the few desires that
remain. Yet I would rather have chilly age than hot youth;
I would rather know that God is near to me now, than
have no thought of him in my head at all. I have enjoyed
my time on earth; now I look forward to eternity in
heaven.

Celtic

O God, as you granted to Simeon and Anna in the evening of their lives to behold the Word made flesh, so grant us each evening to lay down our work in peace, trusting the outcome to your grace and our souls to your loving arms, through Jesus Christ our Salvation. Amen.

Michael Counsell

Nunc Dimittis

LORD, now lettest thou thy servant depart in peace: according to thy word.
For mine eyes have seen thy salvation,
which thou hast prepared before the face of all people;
to be a light to lighten the Gentiles:
and to be the glory of thy people Israel.

Luke 2:29–32

O Lord,
support us all the day long of this troublous life,
until the shades lengthen, and the evening comes,
the busy world is hushed,
the fever of life is over,
and our work is done.
Then Lord in thy mercy
grant us safe lodging,
a holy rest,
and peace at the last,
through Jesus Christ our Lord. Amen.

John Henry Newman

O strength and stay upholding all creation,
  Who ever dost thyself unmoved abide,
Yet day by day the light in due gradation
From hour to hour through all its changes guide;

Grant to life's day a calm unclouded ending,
An eve untouched by shadows of decay,
The brightness of a holy death-bed blending
With dawning glories of the eternal day.

Hear us, O Father, gracious and forgiving,
Through Jesus Christ thy co-eternal Word,
Who with the Holy Ghost by all things living
Now and to endless ages art adored.

Ambrose of Milan

Before Sleep

Repentance

As the evening progresses, the time comes to go to bed. As we look back over the day that is past, we confess how far short we have fallen from the standard of love set for us by the example of Jesus, knowing that only his forgiveness can give us a clear conscience and a good night's sleep.

HOW happy are those whose sins are forgiven,
    for whom atonement is made.
Happy are those whom the Lord does not count as guilty,
and in whose spirit there is no deceit.
I confessed my sin to you,
and I did not conceal my wickedness.
I said, 'I will admit my disobedience to the Lord,'
and you forgave the guilt of my sin.
So let all your people pray to you,
when you may be found.
You are my hiding place;
you keep me safe from trouble;
you surround me with songs of deliverance.

Psalm 32:1–7

GOD in heaven, you have helped my life to grow like a tree. Now, something has happened. Satan, like a bird, has carried in one twig of his own choosing after

43

another. Before I knew it he had built a dwelling place and was living in it. Tonight, my Father, I am throwing out both the bird and the nest.

A Nigerian Christian

SOFTLY now the light of day
Fades upon my sight away;
Free from care, from labour free,
Lord, I would commune with thee.

Thou, whose all-pervading eye
Naught escapes, without, within,
Pardon each infirmity,
Open fault and secret sin.

When for me the light of day
Shall for ever pass away,
Then, from sin and sorrow free,
Take me, Lord, to dwell with thee.

Thou who sinless yet hast known
All of man's infirmity;
Then, from thine eternal throne,
Jesus, look with pitying eye.

George Washington Doane

O great chief, light a candle in my heart, that I may see what is in it, and sweep the rubbish from your dwelling place.

An African schoolgirl

WE have wounded your love:
    O God, heal us.
We stumble in the darkness:
Light of the world, transfigure us.
We forget that we are your home:
Spirit of God, dwell in us.

Jim Cotter

WE repent the wrongs we have done:
    our blindness to human need and suffering;
our indifference to injustice and cruelty;
our false judgments, petty thoughts, and contempt;
our waste and pollution of the earth and oceans;
our lack of concern for those who come after us;
our complicity in the making of weapons of mass
    destruction,
and our threatening their use.

Jim Cotter

ETERNAL Spirit, living God,
    in whom we live and move and have our being,
all that we are, have been, and shall be is known to you,
to the very secrets of our hearts
and all that rises to trouble us.
Living flame, burn into us:
Cleansing wind, blow through us:
Fountain of water, well up within us:
that we may love and praise in deed and in truth.

Jim Cotter

PRAISE the Lord, my soul!
    Let every part of me praise his holy name.
Praise the Lord, my soul!
I will never forget what he has done for me.
He has forgiven all my sins,
and healed all my sickness,
he has brought back my life from disaster,
and crowned me with his loving-kindness.
God satisfies all my desires,
making me young again like an eagle.
God brings justice and victory to all the oppressed.
The Lord is merciful and gracious,
slow to anger and of great mercy;
he will not always punish,
nor does his anger last for ever.
He has not treated us as we deserved,
nor given us the punishment our sins had earned.
As high as the heavens are above the earth,
that is how high God's mercy is
over those who reverence him;
as far as the east is from the west,
that is how far God has separated us from our sins.
Like parents pity their children,
so God pities those who worship him,
for he knows what we are made of;
he remembers that we are only dust.

Psalm 103:1–6, 8–14

THE night is come, like to the day.
    Depart not thou, great God, away.
Let not my sins, black as the night,
Eclipse the lustre of thy light.
Keep still in my horizon; for to me
The sun makes not the day, but thee.

Thou whose nature cannot sleep,
On my temples sentry keep.
Guard me 'gainst those watchful foes,
Whose eyes are open while mine close.
Let no dreams my head infest,
But such as Jacob's temples blest.
While I do rest, my soul advance:
Make my sleep a holy trance:
That I may, my rest being wrought,
Awake into some holy thought,
And with as active vigour run
My course, as doth the nimble sun.
Sleep is a death; O make me try,
By sleeping, what it is to die!
And as gently lay my head
On my grave, as now my bed.
Howe'er I rest, great God, let me
Awake again at last with thee.
And thus assured, behold I lie
Securely, or to wake or die.
These are my drowsy days; in vain
I do now wake to sleep again:
O come that hour, when I shall never
Sleep again, but wake for ever!

Sir Thomas Browne

T HE disciples saw some people carrying a mat with a
paralysed man lying on it. When Jesus saw their
faith, he said to the paralysed man, 'Cheer up, my lad;
your sins have been forgiven.' Immediately, some of the
religious experts started saying among themselves, 'What
this man is saying is blasphemy.' Jesus knew what they
were thinking, and asked them, 'Why do you think these
evil thoughts? Which is easier, to say, "Your sins are

forgiven," or to say, "Stand up and walk"? But listen, then you will know that the Son of Man has authority on earth to forgive sins.' He then said to the paralysed man, 'Stand up, pick up your mat and go home.' The man who had been paralysed then stood up and went home. When the crowd saw it, they were amazed; they praised God, because he had given such authority to human beings.

Matthew 9:2–8

BEFORE we go to rest, we would commit ourselves to God's care through Christ, beseeching him to forgive us for all our sins of this day past, and to keep alive his grace in our hearts, and to cleanse us from all sin, pride, harshness and selfishness, and to give us the spirit of meekness, humility, firmness and love. O Lord, keep thyself present to us ever, and perfect thy strength in our weakness. Take us and ours under thy blessed care, this night and evermore; through Jesus Christ our Lord. Amen.

Thomas Arnold

O eternal God, king of all creation, who brought us to this hour: forgive us the sins which we have committed this day in thought, word and deed, and cleanse, O Lord, our humble souls from every stain of flesh and spirit. Grant us, O Lord, to pass through the sleep of this night in peace, to rise from our beds again to please your holy name all the days of our lives, and to vanquish the enemies, both bodily and spiritual, that contend against us. Deliver us, O Lord, from the vain thoughts that stain us, and from evil desires. For the kingdom, the glory and the power are yours, Father, Son and Holy Spirit, now and for ever and to the ages of ages. Amen.

Macarius the Great

S WEET Saviour, bless us ere we go;
    Thy word into our minds instil,
And make our lukewarm hearts to glow
    With lowly love and fervent will.
Through life's long day and death's dark night;
O gentle Jesus, be our Light.

The day is done, its hours have run,
    And thou hast taken count of all;
The scanty triumphs grace hath won,
    The broken vow, the frequent fall.
Through life's long day and death's dark night;
O gentle Jesus, be our Light.

Grant us, dear Lord, from evil ways
    True absolution and release;
And bless us, more than in past days,
    With purity and inward peace.
Through life's long day and death's dark night;
O gentle Jesus, be our Light.

Do more than pardon; give us joy,
    Sweet fear and sober liberty,
And loving hearts without alloy,
    That only long to be like thee.
Through life's long day and death's dark night;
O gentle Jesus, be our Light.

Labour is sweet, for thou hast toiled,
    And care is light, for thou hast cared;
Let not our works with self be soiled,
    Nor in unsimple ways ensnared.
Through life's long day and death's dark night;
O gentle Jesus, be our Light.

For all we love, the poor, the sad,
    The sinful, – unto thee we call;
Oh let thy mercy make us glad;
    Thou art our Jesus and our All.
Through life's long day and death's dark night;
O gentle Jesus, be our Light.

Frederick William Faber

LOOK down, O Lord, from your heavenly throne, illumine the darkness of this night with your celestial brightness, and from the children of light, banish the deeds of darkness; through Jesus Christ our Lord. Amen.

The Ambrosian Sacramentary

O merciful God, eternal light, shining in darkness, you dispel the night of sin and all blindness of heart. Since you have appointed the night for rest and the day for labour, grant that our bodies may rest in peace and quietness, that afterward they may be able to endure the labour they must bear. Limit our sleep that it may not be excessive, so that we may remain pure both in body and soul, and that our sleep itself may be to your glory. Enlighten the eyes of our understanding, so that we may not sleep in death, but always look for deliverance from this world of misery. Defend us against all assaults of the devil and take us into your holy protection. And although we have not passed this day without greatly sinning against you, we ask you to hide our sins with your mercy, as you hide all things on earth with the darkness of the night, so that we may not be cast out from your presence. Relieve and comfort all who are afflicted in mind, body, or estate. Through Jesus Christ our Lord.

Jean Calvin

FORGIVE me, O God, because of your great mercy;
   your tender mercy is so great:
blot out the record of my sins.
Wash me thoroughly until the stains are gone;
make me clean from all my sin.
For I confess my disobedience;
I can never forget my sin.
It is you, O God, only you, that I have offended;
you have seen the evil.
So, you would be justified in condemning me,
and clear when you judge me.
Look at me! I have been a sinner since my life began,
I was conceived in a world full of sin;
whereas what you require is total truthfulness,
and inner wisdom is what you teach me.
Scour my soul until it is clean;
wash me, till I am pure and shining;
make me hear the sounds of joy and gladness,
so that what was crushed in me may rejoice.
Look away from my sins,
cross out the record of my wrongdoing;
create me a clean heart, dear God,
and renew in me a steadfast spirit.
Open my lips, dear Lord,
then my mouth will proclaim your praise.

Psalm 51:1–11, 15

O God, the Saviour of the living and the dying, pardon
all my offences, I humbly beg of you, both those
committed intentionally and my thoughtless and uninten-
tional faults. When at last you command my soul to
depart from my body, let your holy angels protect my soul
from all evil powers, and carry it safely to your heavenly
kingdom.

The Leonine Sacramentary

GOD, who commanded us to let not the sun go down on our wrath, we confess before you tonight all our sins of hatred, selfishness and pride during the day. As the darkness covers the earth, so may your Son's atoning death cover and blot out all our transgressions. If through your grace we have done any good this day, accept it as our evening sacrifice, and raise us up in the morning to newness of life, through the same Jesus Christ our Lord. Amen.

Michael Counsell

IN God's hands there is nothing wrong with remorse. Remorse can produce repentance which leads to salvation. Without God, however, worldly grief leads only to the death of the soul.

2 Corinthians 7:10

I am taking off my dusty, dirty clothes. In the same way let me be stripped of the sins I have committed today. Dear Lord, I confess that my thoughts and actions have been selfish in many, many ways. Now I stand before you, naked in body and in soul alike, to be washed clean. Let me rest in your arms tonight. Then may my dreams be holy, and may I wake up tomorrow strong and eager to serve you.

Jacob Boehme

The peace of God

Laying the worries of the day one by one to rest, we ask God to flood our hearts with peace.

LORD, I cast all my care on you,
   because you care for me.

Adapted from 1 Peter 5:7

THE Lord almighty grant us a quiet night and peace at the last, through Jesus Christ our Lord.

Compline

REJOICE in the Lord always; and again I say, Rejoice.
Let your reasonableness be known to everyone.
The Lord is near.
Be anxious about nothing,
but in everything, by prayer and supplication
with thanksgiving,
let your requests be made known to God.
And the peace of God,
which surpasses all understanding,
will keep your hearts and minds in Christ Jesus.
Finally, my friends,
whatever is true,
whatever is honourable,
whatever is just,
whatever is pure,
whatever is pleasing,
whatever is commendable,
if there is any excellence,
if there is anything deserving praise,
think about these things.

Philippians 4:6–8

LORD, it is eventide: the light of day is waning;
Far o'er the golden land earth's voices faint and fall;
Lowly we pray to thee for strength and love sustaining,
Lowly we ask of thee thy peace upon us all.
O grant unto our souls
Light that groweth not pale
With day's decrease,
Love that never can fail
Till life shall cease;
Joy no trial can mar,
Hope that shineth afar,
Faith serene as a star,
And Christ's own peace.

Lord, it is eventide: we turn to thee for healing,
Like those of Galilee who came at close of day;
Speak to our waiting souls, their hidden needs revealing;
Touch us with hands divine that take our sin away.
O grant unto our souls
Light that groweth not pale
With day's decrease,
Love that never can fail
Till life shall cease;
Joy no trial can mar,
Hope that shineth afar,
Faith serene as a star,
And Christ's own peace.

Saviour, thou knowest all the trial and temptation,
Knowest the wilfulness and waywardness of youth,
Help us to hold to thee, our strength and our salvation,
Help us to find in thee the one eternal Truth.
O grant unto our souls
Light that groweth not pale
With day's decrease,

Love that never can fail
Till life shall cease;
Joy no trial can mar,
Hope that shineth afar,
Faith serene as a star,
And Christ's own peace.

Lord, it is eventide: our hearts await thy giving,
Wait for that peace divine that none can take away,
Peace that shall lift our souls to loftier heights of living,
Till we abide with thee in everlasting day.
O grant unto our souls
Light that groweth not pale
With day's decrease,
Love that never can fail
Till life shall cease;
Joy no trial can mar,
Hope that shineth afar,
Faith serene as a star,
And Christ's own peace.

H. Ernest Nichol

INTO your arms we now commend ourselves this night. We will lie down in peace, if you speak peace to us through Jesus Christ. May our last thoughts be of you. And when we wake up, may your Spirit bring heavenly things to our mind. Pardon the imperfections of our prayers. Supply what we have omitted to ask for, and do for us 'exceeding abundantly above all that we ask or think'; for the sake of Jesus Christ our Lord. Amen.

Fielding Ould

Going to Rest

MAY the Light of lights come
        To my dark heart from Thy place;
May the Spirit's wisdom come
    To my heart's tablet from my Saviour.

Be the peace of the Spirit mine this night,
Be the peace of the Son mine this night,
Be the peace of the Father mine this night,
The peace of all peace be mine this night,
Each morning and evening of my life.

Carmina Gadelica III, 337

TWILIGHT'S peace and holy calm
        Steals across the earth and skies;
Let glad melodies of praise
To our heavenly Father rise.

As the shades of evening fall
Gently over all the land,
All the seeds we've sown today
We commit unto thy hand.

If within our daily course
Deeds of kindness we have shown,
Let them be like hidden gems,
Unassuming and unknown.

Peace of evening, oh how sweet,
When the birds return to nest,
And when we our footsteps turn
Back towards home and blessed rest.

When at last life's journey ends,
And at last we cease to roam,
May we gaze upon thy face,
Hear thy gracious 'Welcome home'.

Albert A. Bennett

O Lord God, grant us your peace, for you have supplied us with all things – the peace of rest, the peace of the Sabbath, which has no evening; through Jesus Christ our Lord. Amen.

Augustine of Hippo

SAVIOUR, again to thy dear name we raise
With one accord our parting hymn of praise.
Guard thou the lips from sin, the hearts from shame,
That in this house have called upon thy name.

Grant us thy peace, Lord, through the coming night;
Turn thou for us its darkness into light;
From harm and danger keep thy children free,
For dark and light are both alike to thee.

Grant us thy peace throughout our earthly life;
Peace to thy Church from error and from strife;
Peace to our land, the fruit of truth and love;
Peace in each heart, thy Spirit from above:

Thy peace in life, the balm of every pain;
Thy peace in death, the hope to rise again;
Then, when thy voice shall bid our conflict cease,
Call us, O Lord, to thine eternal peace.

John Ellerton

WEARIED by the conflict of life, worn by the burden of the day, we seek you, Lord Jesus, as our resting-place. May your eternal calm descend on our troubled spirits and give us all your peace. Amid the treacherous sands of time you still stand, the Rock of Ages. In life's desert places you are a spring whose waters never fail.

William Orchard

BLESSED are you, O Lord our God, king of the universe; you make the bands of sleep to fall on my eyes, and slumber on my eyelids. May it be your will, O Lord my God and God of my ancestors, to let me lie down in peace and rise up again in peace. Let no troubled thoughts nor bad dreams nor evil desires disturb me, but give me perfect rest in your presence. Lighten mine eyes, lest I sleep the sleep of death, for you give light to the apple of the eye. Blessed are you, O Lord, you give light to the whole world in your glory.

From the Jewish book of Berakoth

DEAR Lord and Father of mankind,
  forgive our foolish ways;
re-clothe us in our rightful mind,
in purer lives thy service find,
in deeper reverence praise.

In simple trust like theirs who heard,
beside the Syrian sea,
the gracious calling of the Lord,
let us, like them, without a word
rise up and follow thee.

O Sabbath rest by Galilee!
O calm of hills above,
where Jesus knelt to share with thee
the silence of eternity,
interpreted by love!

With that deep hush subduing all
Our words and works that drown
The tender whisper of thy call,
As noiseless let thy blessing fall
As fell thy manna down.

Drop thy still dews of quietness,
till all our strivings cease;
take from our souls the strain and stress,
and let our ordered lives confess
the beauty of thy peace;

Breathe through the heats of our desire
thy coolness and thy balm;
let sense be dumb, let flesh retire;
speak through the earthquake, wind, and fire,
O still small voice of calm.

John Greenleaf Whittier

LORD, make me an instrument of your peace.
Where there is hatred let me sow love;
where there is injury, pardon;
where there is discord, union;
where there is doubt, faith;
where there is despair, hope;
where there is darkness, light;
where there is sadness, joy.
Grant that I may seek not so much to be consoled,
    as to console;
to be understood, as to understand;

to be loved, as to love.
For it is by giving that we receive;
it is by losing that we find;
it is by forgiving that we are forgiven;
and it is by dying that we rise again to eternal life,
in Jesus Christ our Lord. Amen.

'The Prayer of Saint Francis'

O God, from whom all holy desires,
all good counsels,
and all just works do proceed;
give unto thy servants that peace which the world cannot
give,
that both, our hearts may be set to obey thy
commandments,
and also that, by thee, we,
being defended from the fear of our enemies,
may pass our time in rest and quietness,
through the merits of Jesus Christ our Saviour. Amen.

The Gelasian Sacramentary

WITH earnest prayer
we ask for the angel of peace and mercy,
from you, O Lord.
Night and day throughout our life,
we ask for continued peace for your Church,
from you, O Lord.
We ask for continual love,
which is the perfect bond of unity,
confirmed by the Holy Spirit,
from you, O Lord.
We ask for forgiveness of sins and those things
which help our lives and bring pleasure to you,
from you, O Lord.

We ask the mercy and compassion of the Lord
    continually and at all times,
    from you, O Lord.

The Nestorian Evening Office

I watched her in the loud and shadowy lanes
    Of life; and every face that passed her by
Grew calmly restful, smiling quietly,
As though she gave, for all their griefs and pains,
Largesse of comfort, soft as summer rains,
And balsam tinctured with tranquillity,
Yet in her own eyes dwelt an agony.
'Oh, halcyon soul!' I cried, 'what sorrow reigns
In that calm heart which knows such ways to heal?'
She said – 'Where balms are made for human uses,
Great furnace fires, and wheel on grinding wheel
Must crush and purify the crude herb juices,
And in some hearts the conflicts never cease;
They are the sick world's factories of peace.'

Mary Webb

Faith and confidence in God

*Peace comes when we realise that we do not have to
control the future, but can trust God to meet all our
needs.*

I lie down and go to sleep,
    and all night long the Lord protects me.
I am not afraid of all the many enemies
who surround me wherever I go.

Psalm 3:5–6

GOD is our refuge and strength,
a very present help in trouble.
Taste and see how good the Lord is;
happy are those who trust in him.

Psalms 46:1; 34:8

I seek a hiding place in you, dear Lord;
never let me feel disappointed; rescue me in triumph.
Graciously hear me; deliver me quickly;
be like a strong rock for me to hide in,
a mighty fortress to save me.
You, you are my rock and my fortress;
lead me and guide me for the sake of your good name.
Cut me out of the net that I am trapped in,
only you are strong enough to do it.
Into your hands I commend my spirit,
for you have redeemed me,
you, the trustworthy Lord God.

Psalm 31:1–5

FAITH is the certainty that we shall receive the things
we hope for, the conviction that the things we cannot
see really do exist. It was by their faith that our ancestors
received God's approval.

Hebrews 11:1–2

LORD, when we sleep let us not be made afraid,
but let our sleep be sweet,
that we may be enabled to serve thee on the morrow,
through Jesus Christ our Lord. Amen.

William Laud

HUSHED was the evening hymn,
  The temple courts were dark,
The lamp was burning dim
Before the sacred ark:
When suddenly a voice divine
Rang through the silence of the shrine.

The old man, meek and mild,
The priest of Israel, slept;
His watch the temple child,
The little Levite, kept;
And what from Eli's sense was sealed
The Lord to Hannah's son revealed.

O give me Samuel's ear!
The open ear, O Lord;
Alive and quick to hear
Each whisper of thy word;
Like him to answer at thy call
and to obey thee first of all.

O give me Samuel's heart!
A lowly heart that waits
Where in thy house thou art,
Or watches at thy gates,
By day and night, a heart that still
Moves at the breathing of thy will.

O give me Samuel's mind!
A sweet unmurmuring faith,
Obedient and resigned
To thee – in life and death;
That I may read with child-like eyes
Truths that are hidden from the wise.

James Drummond Burns

O Lord God,
  in whom we live and move and have our being,
open our eyes that we may behold
    thy fatherly presence ever about us.
Draw our hearts to thee with the power of love.
Teach us in nothing to be anxious;
and when we have done what thou hast given us to do,
help us, O God our Saviour,
to leave the issue to thy wisdom.
Take from us all doubt and distrust.
Lift our thoughts up to thee,
and make us know that all things are possible to us,
in and through thy Son our redeemer,
    Jesus Christ our Lord. Amen.

Brooke Foss Westcott

PAUL and Silas were singing hymns to you during the
    night,
and so the Philippian jailer was brought to faith.
Lord Jesus, may we bear witness by our faith in you
even in the darkest hours.

Michael Counsell

THE sun has disappeared.
   I have turned off the light,
and my wife and children are asleep.
The animals in the forest are full of fear;
they prefer the day with your sun to the night.
But I know that your moon is still there,
and your eyes and also your hands.
Thus I am not afraid.
This day again
you led me wonderfully.
Everybody went to their mat
satisfied and full.

Renew us during our sleep,
that in the morning
we may come afresh to our daily work.

A Ghanaian Christian

LORD God, you have given us the night for rest. I pray that while I sleep my soul may remain awake to you, holding fast to your love. As I lay aside my worries, to relax and refresh my mind, may I not forget your infinite and unresting care for me. So let my conscience be at peace; then when I arise tomorrow, I shall be refreshed in body, mind and soul.

Jean Calvin

WATCH over us as we rest, O God, as a mother tends her sleeping children. Grant us the perfect peace of those whose minds are fixed on you, and the assurance of your love, that we may awake with body, mind and soul refreshed, through Jesus Christ our Lord. Amen.

Michael Counsell

HOW weak the thoughts and vain
    Of self-deluding men!
Men, who fixed to earth alone
Think their houses shall endure,
Fondly call their lands their own,
To their distant heirs secure!

How happy then are we,
Who build, O Lord, on thee!
What can our foundation shock?
Though the shattered earth remove,
Stands our city on a rock,
On the rock of heavenly love.

A house we call our own,
Which cannot be o'erthrown:
In the general ruin sure,
Storms and earthquakes it defies,
Built immovably secure,
Built eternal in the skies.

Charles Wesley

LORD Christ, you are awaked as a giant out of sleep to be the resurrection and the life of all who have faith in you: grant us the sleep of the justified this night, that whether it be in this life or on the shores of eternity, we may find you there to welcome us when we awake, our Saviour, our Master, and our Friend for ever. Amen.

Michael Counsell

SOMETIMES a light surprises
The Christian while he sings;
It is the Lord who rises
With healing in His wings:
When comforts are declining
He grants the soul again
A season of clear shining
To cheer it after rain.

In holy contemplation
We sweetly then pursue
The theme of God's salvation,
And find it ever new:
Set free from present sorrow,
We cheerfully can say,
E'en let the unknown to-morrow
Bring with it what it may,

66

It can bring with it nothing
But he will bear us through;
Who gives the lilies clothing,
Will clothe his people too;
Beneath the spreading heavens
No creature but is fed;
And he who feeds the ravens
Will give his children bread.

Though vine nor fig-tree neither
Their wonted fruit shall bear;
Though all the field should wither,
Nor flocks nor herds be there;
Yet, God the same abiding,
His praise shall tune my voice;
For, while in Him confiding,
I cannot but rejoice.

William Cowper

THERE'S a wideness in God's mercy
    Like the wideness of the sea;
There's a kindness in his justice,
    Which is more than liberty.

There is no place where earth's sorrows
    Are more felt than up in heaven;
There is no place where earth's failings
    Have such kindly judgement given.

There is grace enough for thousands
    Of new worlds as great as this;
There is room for fresh creations
    In that upper home of bliss.

For the love of God is broader
    Than the measures of man's mind;
And the heart of the Eternal
    Is most wonderfully kind.

But we make his love too narrow
    By false limits of our own;
And we magnify his strictness
    With a zeal he will not own.

There is plentiful redemption
    In the blood that has been shed,
There is joy for all the members
    In the sorrows of the Head.

'Tis not all we owe to Jesus;
    It is something more than all;
Greater good because of evil,
    Larger mercy through the fall.

If our love were but more simple,
    We should take him at his word;
And our lives would be all sunshine
    In the sweetness of our Lord.

Frederick William Faber

THE Lord is my shepherd;
    I shall lack nothing.
He lets me lie in green pastures;
he leads me to restful waters.
He refreshes my life;
he guides me in paths of righteousness.
Even when I walk through valleys of deep darkness,
I am not afraid;
for you, Lord, are with me;
your shepherd's crook and staff reassure me.

You have laid a banquet before me,
in the presence of my enemies;
you have anointed my head with oil;
my cup is full to the brim.
Goodness and mercy will follow me,
all the days of my life,
and I will live in the Lord's house for ever.

Psalm 23

Protection

If we will trust him, God will protect us from all dangers.

I will lie down in peace, and take my rest;
for you, Lord, only, can cause me to live in safety.

Psalm 4:9

I look ahead to the hills;
where shall I find strength?
My help comes from the Lord,
the maker of heaven and earth.
He will not let me stumble;
he watches over me unsleeping;
God, who watches over his people,
never sleeps.
The Lord protects me;
the Lord shades me from the eastern sun;
I shall not get sunstroke by day,
nor moonstruck by night.
The Lord will protect me from all evil;
he will protect my life.
The Lord will protect me as I go out and come home,
now and forever.

Psalm 121

HE said not: *Thou shalt not be tempested, thou shalt not be travailed, thou shalt not be afflicted*; but he said: *Thou shalt not be overcome*. God willeth that we take heed to these words, and that we be ever strong in sure trust, in weal and woe. For he loveth and enjoyeth us, and so willeth he that we love and enjoy him and mightily trust in him; and *all shall be well*.

Julian of Norwich

SAVIOUR, breathe an evening blessing,
Ere repose our spirits seal;
Sin and want we come confessing;
Thou canst save, and thou canst heal.

Though the night be dark and dreary,
Darkness cannot hide from thee;
Thou art he who, never weary,
Watchest where thy people be.

Though destruction walk around us,
Though the arrows past us fly,
Angel-guards from thee surround us;
We are safe, if thou art nigh.

Be thou nigh, should death o'ertake us;
Jesus, then our refuge be,
And in paradise awake us,
There to rest in peace with thee.

James Edmeston

NOW the day is over,
  Night is drawing nigh,
Shadows of the evening
Steal across the sky.

Jesus, give the weary
Calm and sweet repose;
With thy tenderest blessings
May our eyelids close.

Comfort every sufferer
Watching late in pain;
Those who plan some evil
From their sin restrain.

Through the long night watches
May thine angels spread
Their white wings above me,
Watching round my bed.

When the morning wakens,
Then may I arise
Pure, and fresh, and sinless
In thy holy eyes.

Sabine Baring-Gould

LIGHTEN our darkness,
  we beseech thee, O Lord;
and by thy great mercy defend us
  from all perils and dangers of this night;
for the love of thy only Son,
our Saviour, Jesus Christ. Amen.

The Gelasian Sacramentary

THE day is past and over;
  All thanks, O Lord, to thee;
I pray thee that offenceless
The hours of dark may be:
O Jesu, keep me in thy sight,
And guard me through the coming night.

The joys of day are over;
I lift my heart to thee,
And call on thee that sinless
The hours of dark may be:
O Jesu, make their darkness light,
And guard me through the coming night.

The toils of day are over;
I raise the hymn to thee,
And ask that free from peril
The hours of dark may be:
O Jesu, keep me in thy sight,
And guard me through the coming night

Be thou my soul's preserver,
O God! for thou dost know
How many are the perils
Through which I have to go:
Lover of souls! O hear my call,
And guard and save me from them all.

John Mason Neale

CONTINUE thy gracious protection to us, Lord,
  this night. Defend us from all dangers, and from the
fear of them, that we may enjoy such refreshing sleep as
may fit us for the duties of the coming day. And grant us
grace always to live so close to thee that we may never be

afraid to die, so that, living or dying, we may be completely thine, in Jesus Christ our Lord. Amen.

Edmund Gibson

B EFORE the ending of the day,
Creator of the world, we pray
That with thy wonted favour thou
Wouldst be our guard and keeper now.

From all ill dreams defend our eyes,
From nightly fears and fantasies;
Tread under foot our ghostly foe,
That no pollution we may know.

O Father, that we ask be done,
Through Jesus Christ, thine only Son;
Who, with the Holy Ghost and thee,
Doth live and reign eternally. Amen.

John Mason Neale

B LESSED are you, Almighty Master, you have
allowed us to pass through this day and to reach the
beginning of the night. Hear our prayers, and those of all
your people; forgive us our sins, voluntary and involuntary, and accept our evening supplications. Send down on
your people the fullness of your mercy and compassion.
Surround us with your holy angels, arm us with the
armour of your righteousness, fence us round with your
truth, guard us with your power. Deliver us from every
attack and every trick of Satan our enemy, and grant us to
pass this evening and the ensuing night, and all the days of
our life, in fullness of peace and holiness, without sin and
stumbling. For it is your nature to pity and to save, O
Christ our God. Amen.

Orthodox

IN the evening and morning and at noon we praise you;
we thank you, and pray to you, Master of all,
to direct our prayers so that they rise like incense before
you.
Do not allow our hearts to turn away
to words or thoughts of wickedness,
but keep us from all things that might hurt us.
Our eyes look up to you, Lord, and in you we hope:
never let us be defeated,
for the sake of Jesus Christ our Lord. Amen.

Orthodox

NOW that evening has fallen,
To God, the Creator, I will turn in prayer,
Knowing that he will help me.
I know the Father will help me.

From the Dinka people, Sudan

Nada Te Turbe

LET nothing disturb you;
nothing dismay you;
all things pass,
but God never changes.
Whoever has God lacks nothing:
if you have only God, you have more than enough.

Teresa of Avila

Ein Feste Burg

A safe stronghold our God is still,
A trusty shield and weapon;
He'll help us clear from all the ill
That hath us now o'ertaken.

The ancient prince of hell
Hath risen with purpose fell;
Strong mail of craft and power
He weareth in this hour.
On earth is not his fellow.

With force of arms we nothing can,
Full soon were we down-ridden;
But for us fights the proper Man,
Whom God himself hath bidden.
Ask ye, who is this same?
Christ Jesus is his name,
The Lord Sabaoth's Son;
He, and no other one,
Shall conquer in the battle.

Martin Luther

A Riddle

ETERNAL the creator who rules the world,
whose power sustains and governs the earth.
Mighty the king, monarch and master of all;
ruler and guide of heaven and earth,
holding them all in his embrace.
In the beginning, when God founded the earth, he
    created me,
he told me to stay awake, and never sleep again.
The omnipotent Creator guides the world,
and by his word I encompass the whole earth.
So timid am I that a ghost can frighten me;
Yet as bold as a boar of the forest
who crouches at bay, furious with rage.
No earthly warrior can overpower me,
Only God, who rules the highest heavens.

The Exeter Book

DEAR King, my own King, no pride or sin have you:
you created the universe, eternal, conquering
King.
Higher than nature, higher than the sun, deeper than the
ocean:
King of north, south, east and west; no enemy can
conquer you.
Mysterious King, you existed before anything:
before the sun was placed in the sky,
before the waters filled the ocean:
King of beauty, without beginning or end.
King, you made dark and light:
not proud or boastful, but strong and firm.
King, you moulded the earth from chaos:
carved out the mountains and dug the valleys,
and covered the earth with grass and trees.
King, you stretched out the round heavens:
perfect as a hollowed-out fruit,
and spangled them with bright stars at night.
King, you pour pure water from the springs:
to cover the land with streams and rivers.
King, you made the eight winds:
to blow from the points of the compass and swirl
around.
The north wind is white with winter snow:
the south wind is warm and ruddy;
the west wind is a cool blue breeze on the sea:
the east wind is yellow and treacherous;
the lesser winds blow green, orange, mauve and black:
the black wind blows in the dark of the night.
King, you measured the dimensions of creation:
high mountains, deep oceans, sun to moon and star to
star;

you told them the way each should travel:
    the sun to cross the sky by day and the moon by night,
the clouds to bring the rain from the sea:
    and the river to carry the water back again.
King, you made cold arctic and hot desert lands:
    and between them cool, wet and fertile,
and you created men and women to care for the earth:
    and praise you for your boundless love.

Oengus the Culdee

ALL praise to God
    when time begins
and at its end,
No matter who seeks God
He will not turn them away
He will not reject them.

The Black Book of Carmarthen

Prayer

FATHER, bless me in my body,
    Father, bless me in my soul;
Father, bless me this night
    In my body and in my soul.

Father, bless me in my life,
    Father, bless me in my creed;
Father, bless me in my tie
    To my life and to my creed.

Father, sanctify to me my speech,
    Father, sanctify to me my heart;
Father, sanctify to me every whit
    In my speech and in my heart.

Carmina Gadelica III, 349

Resting Blessing

IN name of the Lord Jesus,
   And of the Spirit of healing balm,
In name of the Father of Israel,
   I lay me down to rest.

If there be evil threat or quirk,
Or covert act intent on me,
God, free me and encompass me,
   And drive from me mine enemy.

In name of the Father precious,
And of the Spirit of healing balm,
In name of the Lord Jesus,
   I lay me down to rest.

* * *

God, help me and encompass me,
   From this hour till the hour of my death.

Carmina Gadelica I, 79

The Gifts of the Three

SPIRIT, give me of Thine abundance,
   Father, give me of Thy wisdom,
Son, give me in my need,
   Jesus beneath the shelter of Thy shield.

I lie down to-night,
With the Triune of my strength,
With the Father, with Jesus,
   With the Spirit of might.

Carmina Gadelica I, 75

B LESSING and honour, thanksgiving and praise
   more than we can utter, more than we can conceive,
   be unto thee,
O most adorable Trinity, Father, Son, and Holy Ghost,
by all angels, all men, all creatures,
for ever and ever. Amen and Amen.
To God the Father, who first loved us,
and made us accepted in the Beloved:
To God the Son, who loved us,
and washed us from our sins in His own blood:
To God the Holy Ghost,
who sheds the love of God abroad in our hearts
be all love and all glory for time and eternity. Amen.

Thomas Ken

A LONE with none but you, my God,
   I ventured on my way.
What need I fear when you are near,
   O king of night and day?
More safe am I within your hand
   than if a host did round me stand.

St Columba

M AY the Lord bless you and protect you.
   May the Lord look favourably on you,
and be gracious to you.
May the Lord look on you with love,
and give you his peace.

Numbers 6:24–26

An Order for Compline

(a late evening service)

THE Lord Almighty grant us a quiet night and a perfect end.
Amen.

MY friends, be sensible, be careful; because your enemy the Devil, like a roaring lion, prowls around, looking for someone to devour: resist him, firm in the faith.

1 Peter 5:8–9

BUT you, Lord, will have mercy upon us;
Thanks be to God.
Dear God, speedily save us;
Dear Lord, make haste to help us.
Glory to the Father, and to the Son: and to the Holy Spirit;
As it was in the beginning, is now, and shall be for ever.
Alleluia.

Now a Psalm or Psalms may be said, either Psalm 4; Psalm 31:1–6; Psalm 91; Psalm 134; or one of the other Psalm extracts in this book.

YOU Lord, are in the midst of us, and we are called by your name. Do not leave us, dear Lord, our God.
Thanks be to God.

Jeremiah 14:9

INTO your hands, Lord, I commend my spirit;
For you have redeemed me, Lord God of truth.

Now a Hymn may be sung or said, either 'Before the ending of the day' (see page 73) or one of the other hymns in this book.

KEEP me as the apple of your eye;
Hide me under the shadow of your wings.
Preserve us, Lord, waking, and guard us sleeping,
that awake we may watch with Christ,
and asleep we may rest in peace.

Now Nunc Dimittis may be sung or said, in the traditional form (see page 41) or as follows:

MASTER, who repeated
promise of release:
all my tasks completed,
let me leave in peace.

That we've seen salvation
could not be denied:
light for every nation,
and your people's pride.

Glory to the Father,
glory to the Son,
glory, Holy Spirit.
Heaven has begun!*

* This version by Michael Counsell

PRESERVE us, Lord, waking, and guard us sleeping,
   that awake we may watch with Christ,
   and asleep we may rest in peace.

Now the Apostles' Creed may be said:

I believe in God, the Father almighty,
   creator of heaven and earth.

I believe in Jesus Christ, his only Son, our Lord.
He was conceived by the power of the Holy Spirit,
and born of the Virgin Mary.
He suffered under Pontius Pilate,
was crucified, died, and was buried.
He descended to the dead.
On the third day he rose again.
He ascended into heaven,
and is seated at the right hand of the Father.
He will come again to judge the living and the dead.

I believe in the Holy Spirit,
the holy catholic Church,
the communion of saints,
the forgiveness of sins,
the resurrection of the body,
and the life everlasting. Amen.†

LORD, have mercy upon us.
   Christ, have mercy upon us.
Lord, have mercy upon us.

*Now may follow the Lord's Prayer, in any familiar
translation.*

† This version by the International Consultation on English
Texts

LET us praise the Lord, the God of our ancestors;
Let us praise and glorify him above all for ever.
Let us praise the Father, the Son, and the Holy Spirit;
Let us praise him and magnify him for ever.
Let us praise the Lord of heaven and earth;
Let us praise and glorify him above all for ever.
May the almighty and most merciful Lord
guard us and give us his blessing.
Amen.

WE confess to God Almighty,
the Father, the Son, and the Holy Spirit,
that we have sinned in thought, word, and deed,
and it was our own fault.
So we ask God to have mercy upon us.
Almighty God, have mercy upon us,
forgive us all our sins and deliver us from all evil,
confirm and strengthen us in all goodness,
and bring us to eternal life;
through Jesus Christ our Lord. Amen.

MAY the Almighty and merciful Lord grant *us/you*
pardon and remission of all *our/your* sins,
time for amendment of life,
and the grace and comfort of the Holy Spirit.
Amen.

WILL you not return and give us life;
That your people may rejoice in you?
Lord, shew your mercy upon us;
And grant us your salvation.
Lord, keep us this night without sin;
Lord, have mercy upon us, have mercy upon us.
Lord, hear our prayer;
And let our cry come before you.
Let us pray.

Now a prayer or prayers from this book may be said.

WE will lie down in peace and take our rest;
    For you, Lord, only can cause us to dwell in
      safety.
The Lord be with you;
And also with you.
Let us bless the Lord;
Thanks be to God.
The almighty and merciful Lord,
the Father, the Son, and the Holy Spirit,
bless and preserve us.
Amen.

Intimacy and Ecstasy

The night is a time for love, and many prayers address God as 'Lover', 'Love' or 'the Beloved'. It is a time of creativity and conception of life, and human love should also be celebrated in our thanksgivings to God.

CHILDREN are a gift from the Lord,
  their conception a reward from God;
happy are those who have children;
they hold up their heads with pride.

Psalm 127:4, 6

Love True and Ever Green

ALL other love is like the moon
  That waxeth or waneth as flower in plain,
As flower that blooms and fadeth soon,
As day that showereth and ends in rain.

All other love begins with bliss,
In weeping and woe makes its ending;
No love there is that's our whole bliss
But that which rests on heaven's king.

Anonymous (c. 1350)

I'LL come to thee at eventide
 When the west is streaked wi' grey
I'll wish the night thy charms to hide
And daylight all away.

I'll come to thee at set o' sun
Where white thorns i' the May
I'll come to thee when work is done
And love thee till the day.

When daisy stars are all turned green
And all is meadow grass
I'll wander down the bank at e'en
And court the bonny lass.

The green banks and the rustling sedge
I'll wander down at e'en
All sloping to the water's edge
And in the water green.

And there's the luscious meadow sweet
Beside the meadow drain
My lassie there I once did meet
Who I wish to meet again.

The water lilies were in flower
The yellow and the white
I met her there at even's hour
And stood for half the night.

We stood and loved in that green place
When Sunday's sun got low
Its beams reflected in her face
The fairest thing below.

My sweet Ann Foot my bonny Ann
The meadow banks are green
Meet me at even when you can
Be mine as you have been.

John Clare

S HE walks in beauty, like the night
  Of cloudless climes and starry skies;
And all that's best of dark and bright
Meet in her aspect and her eyes:
Thus mellowed to that tender light
Which heaven to gaudy day denies.

One shade the more, one ray the less,
Had half-impair'd the nameless grace
Which waves in every raven tress,
Or softly lightens o'er her face;
Where thoughts serenely sweet express
How pure, how dear their dwelling place.

And on that cheek, and o'er that brow,
So soft, so calm, yet eloquent,
The smiles that win, the tints that glow,
But tell of days in goodness spent,
A mind at peace with all below,
A heart whose love is innocent.

Lord Byron

W ESTERN wind, when wilt thou blow,
  The small rain down can rain?
Christ, if my love were in my arms
And I in my bed again!

Anonymous (c. 1500)

Nocturne (to Heloïse, from the monastery of St Gildas, Brittany, c. 1136)

THE sea forever drives his weary herd
   Stumbling home to the shore;
The dusk is lonely with a calling bird.
God's gradual hands fling out the stars once more,
Like stone on shining stone,
Till heaven seems over-strewn. . . .
And now my soul calls, troublous and alone.

Now would I have you, silent, at my side,
Your speaking hands in mine,
Gathered beneath the dark wings folding wide,
With all love's glory – human, half-divine –
What was, and what shall be,
Kindled in the eternity
Of one hour's calm by this wild sundering sea.

Peter Abelard

LORD, you are my Lover, it is you whom I desire. You
flow through my body like a stream, you shine on my
face like the sun. Let me be your reflection.

Mechtild of Magdeburg

ONLY if you lead me, Lord, can I join in the dance. If
you want me to, I can leap for joy. But first, you must
dance and sing yourself, to show me how to dance and
sing with you. Together with you, I will dance towards
love; from love I will dance towards truth, and from truth
I will dance towards joy. After that I shall dance beyond
all human senses. I will stay there and dance for ever.

Mechtild of Magdeburg

LORD, love me deeply, love me often, love me long!
The more often you love me, the more pure I
become.
The deeper you love me, the more beautiful I become.
The longer you love me, the holier I become.

Mechtild of Magdeburg

AH, dear love of God,
always hold my soul in your embrace,
for it hurts me more than anything else
to be separated from you.
Ah love, never let me grow cool,
for nothing I do has any life in it
when I can no longer feel your presence.
Oh love, both suffering and poverty are made sweet
when we share them with you;
you teach and comfort the true children of God.

Mechtild of Magdeburg

JESUS, Lover dear and fair,
Sweet thou art beyond compare.

Thou, O Love, wilt never leave us:
Though we sin, wilt never leave us,
Crowned with glory wilt receive us,
If our lot we humbly bear.

Sweet, O Love, so sweet thou art!
Towards thy realm aspires my heart;
Thirst and hunger straight depart,
Love, when once I taste thy fare.

On the Cross thou once didst show,
Love, that thou couldst love us so
That for us thou wast brought low,
Crucified in anguish there.

Thou art Love and Courtesy,
Nought ungracious dwells in thee;
Give, O Love, thyself to me,
Lest I perish in despair!

Jacopone da Todi

LOVE, Love, O Love, thy touch so quickens me,
    Love, Love, O Love, I am no longer I:
Love, Love, O Love, thyself so utterly
    Thou giv'st me, Jesu, that I can but die.
Love, O Love, I am possessed of thee,
    Love, Love, my Love, O take me in a sigh!
    Love, glad and spent I lie.
        O Love, my Bliss,
        O Lover's Kiss!
    O quench my soul in Love!

Jacopone da Todi

LONG and perilous are the paths by which the Lover
seeks his Beloved. They are peopled by cares, sighs
and tears. They are lit up by love.

Many Lovers came together to love One only, their
Beloved, who made them all to abound in love. And each
declared his Beloved perfection, and his thoughts of Him
were very pleasant, making him to suffer pain which
brought delight.

The Lover wept and said, 'How long shall it be till the
darkness of the world is past, that the mad rush of men
towards hell may cease? When comes the hour in which

water, that flows downwards, shall change its nature and mount upwards? When shall the innocent be more in number than the guilty? Ah! When shall the Lover with joy lay down his life for the Beloved? And when shall the Beloved see the Lover grow faint for love of Him?'

The Lover entered a delightful meadow, and saw in the meadow many children who were pursuing butterflies, and trampling down the flowers; and, the more the children laboured to catch the butterflies, the higher did these fly. And the Lover, as he watched them, said: 'Such are they who with subtle reasoning attempt to comprehend the Beloved, who opens the doors to the simple and closes them to the subtle. And Faith reveals the secrets of the Beloved through the casement of love.'

'Say, Fool of Love, why dost thou not speak, and what is this for which thou art thoughtful and perplexed?' The Lover answered: 'I am thinking of the beauties of my Beloved, and the likeness between the bliss and the sorrow which are brought me by the gifts of Love.'

'Say, Fool, which was in being first, thy heart or thy love?' He answered and said: 'Both came into being together; for were it not so, the heart had not been made for love, nor love for reflection.'

Love called his lovers, and bade them ask of him the most desirable and pleasing gifts. And they asked of Love that he would clothe and adorn them after his own manner, that they might be more acceptable to the Beloved.

The Lover cried aloud to all men, and said: 'Love bids you ever love: in walking and sitting, in sleeping and waking, in buying and selling, in weeping and laughing, in speech and in silence, in gain and in loss – in short, in whatsoever you do, for this is Love's commandment.'

Ramón Lull

MY beloved is mine and I am his;
  he pastures his flock among the lilies.
Until the first breath of the breezes of dawn
  when the shadows flee away,
  stay here, my beloved;
leap like a young gazelle or a stag
  on the cleft of the mountains.
Night after night on my bed I dreamt of the love of my life;
  I sought him, but could not find him;
  I called him, but he gave no answer.
'Now I will get up,' I said,
  'and search all over the city;
in the streets and the squares,
  I will look for the love of my life.'
  I sought him, but could not find him.
The city guards found me,
  as they patrolled the city.
  'Have you seen the love of my life?' I asked them.
No sooner had I left them than I found him;
  I found the love of my life.
I held him, and would not let him go
  until I brought him into my mother's house,
  into the room of her that conceived me.
Swear to me, women of Jerusalem,
  by the young gazelle and the doe,
  that you will not interrupt our love.

Song of Songs 2:16 – 3:5

The Virgin Mary's Song at the Conception of Jesus

HAVE you ever felt, on a summer night,
    as though washed in the love divine,
when the stars shine bright with a special light
and you're drunk, but not with wine?
That's how it was on the night when the dove
of the Holy Spirit came
to win my will and my womb from above,
with grace like a burning flame.
The moon filled the room with a subtle shine
of purest, cleanest white;
I lay alone, no joy like mine,
while my depth was swamped with God's height.
And that's how it came that the secret name
of the child I conceived is Love.

Michael Counsell

Healing Sleep

As we abandon ourselves to sleep, we remember that God gave us this precious gift so that our bodies might heal and repair the stresses and wounds of the day. We can let go of the cares and worries which occupy our waking thoughts, as we pursue our journey into God.

Anthem for the Evening

SLEEP, downy sleep, come close my eyes,
Tired with beholding vanities.
Sweet slumbers come, and chase away
The toils and follies of the day;
On your soft bosom will I lie,
Forget the world, and learn to die.
O Israel's watchful Shepherd, spread
Tents of angels round my bed;
Let not the spirits of the air,
While I slumber, me ensnare;
But save thy suppliant free from harms,
Clasped in thine everlasting Arms.
Clouds and thick darkness is thy throne,
Thy wonderful pavilion:
Oh dart from thence a shining ray,
And then my midnight shall be day.
Thus when the morn in crimson drest
Breaks through the windows of the East,
My hymns of thankful praises shall arise
Like incense or the morning sacrifice.

Thomas Flatman

O Lord our God, refresh us with quiet sleep when we are wearied with the day's labour, that, being assisted with the help which our weakness needs, we may be devoted to you both in body and mind; through Jesus Christ our Lord. Amen.

The Leonine Sacramentary

O God of wholeness, we rest in you.
You listen with us to the sound of running water,
you sit with us under the shade of the trees of our healing,
you walk once more with us in the garden in the cool of
  the day,
the oil of your anointing penetrates the cells of our being,
the warmth of your hands steadies us and gives us
  courage.
O God of wholeness, we rest in you.

Jim Cotter

INTO thy hands, most blessed Jesus, I commend my soul and body, for thou hast redeemed both by thy most precious blood. So bless and sanctify my sleep to me, that it may be temperate, holy, and safe, a refreshment to my weary body, to enable it so to serve my soul, that both may serve thee with never-failing duty. Visit, I beseech thee, O Lord, this habitation with thy mercy, and me with thy grace and favour. Teach me to number my days, that I may apply my heart unto wisdom, and ever be mindful of my last end.

Jeremy Taylor

Comfort in grief

Especially in need of healing are those who grieve because of loss. The lonely night is hard to bear, but we can share it with a God who understands our grief, because he too has watched his Son die; and we can share it with Jesus, who wept for the death of his friend.

WEEPING may last for a night,
    but joy comes with the morning.

Psalm 30:5

HOW happy are those who make you their strength:
    your pilgrim paths are in their hearts.
Passing through the valley of weeping,
they turn it into a fountain;
and the gentle rain fills the pools.
They go from strength to strength,
until in Zion they appear before God.

Psalm 84:5–7

CONCERNING my poor dear babe . . . truly I grieved, and felt more than ever I felt before of that grief, which springs from being bereaved of one much beloved: and my heart bleeds, if I may thus speak, at every remembrance of her. But I do not *grieve as one without hope*: hope of meeting her in glory, and spending a joyful eternity together – I do not grieve so as to indulge grief or complaining, or think (with Jonah) *I do well to be angry*, because my darling gourd is withered. God hath done well, and wisely, and graciously; and, whilst my heart is pained, my judgement is satisfied.

Thomas Scott

TO me who am left to mourn his departure, grant that I may not sorrow as one without hope for my beloved who sleeps in thee; but that, always remembering his courage, and the love that united us on earth, I may begin again with new courage to serve thee more fervently who art the only source of true love and true fortitude; that, when I have passed a few more days in this valley of tears and in this shadow of death, supported by thy rod and staff, I may see him again, face to face, in those pastures and amongst those waters of comfort where, I trust, he already walks with thee. Oh Shepherd of the Sheep, have pity upon this darkened soul of mine!

Richard Meux Benson

THERE is time of weeping and there is time of laughing. But as you see, he setteth the weeping time before, for that is the time of this wretched world and the laughing time shall come after in heaven. There is also a time of sowing, and a time of reaping too. Now must we in this world sow, that we may in the other world reap: and in this short sowing time of this weeping world, must we water our seed with the showers of our tears, and then shall we have in heaven a merry laughing harvest for ever.

Sir Thomas More

JESUS told them plainly, 'Lazarus has died.'
Then, as he saw Mary and the people of Judea who had come with her weeping, he groaned deeply and was distressed.
'Where have you put him?' Jesus asked.
'Come and see,' they replied.
Jesus wept.

John 11:14, 33–35

HE was despised and rejected by all,
a man of sorrows, and acquainted with grief.

YOURS is the day, O Lord, and yours is the night.
Grant that the Sun of Righteousness may abide in our
hearts to drive away the darkness of evil thoughts.

The Gelasian Sacramentary

COME, O soul that weepest,
let thy Saviour know;
when thy grief is deepest
tell him all thy woe.
To thy Lord address it,
let thy grief outpour;
fearlessly confess it,
trust, and weep no more.

Tell it to thy Brother,
leave it in his hands;
more than any other
Jesus understands.
Jesus will uphold thee
when thy heart is sore;
think what he has told thee,
trust, and weep no more.

Tell all who are grieving
Christ can bring release;
bring them home, believing,
to the Prince of Peace.
Calm their anxious fears, then,
point them to their Lord;
wipe away their tears – then
thou shalt weep no more.

The French Reformed Hymnal

98

Sleep, a foretaste of death and resurrection

We sink peacefully into sleep, then after a time in which we are unaware of our body, we awake the next day the same person, with the same memories, as we were the night before. This nightly miracle has led many to see sleep as a parable of dying and rising again.

LOOK at me, Lord! Answer me, my God;
restore the glint to my eyes,
don't let me sleep the sleep of death!

Psalm 13:3

JESUS said to them, 'Our friend Lazarus has fallen
asleep. But I am going to wake him up.'

John 11:11

GOD, our loving Father, hear us,
Bless us in our prayers tonight;
Through the darkness be thou near us
Keep us safe till morning light.

All our life thy hand hath led us,
And we thank thee for thy care;
Thou hast warmed and clothed and fed us
Listen to our evening prayer.

May our sins be all forgiven,
Bless the friends we love so well;
Take us when we die to heaven,
Happy there with thee to dwell.

Mary L. Duncan

NOW I lay me down to sleep;
I pray the Lord my soul to keep.
If I should die before I wake,
I pray the Lord my soul to take.

New England Primer

NO man is an island, entire of itself; every man is a
piece of the continent, a part of the main. If a clod
be washed away by the sea, Europe is the less, as well as if
a promontory were, as well as if a manor of thy friend's or
of thine own were: any man's death diminishes me,
because I am involved in mankind, and therefore never
send to know for whom the bell tolls; it tolls for thee.

John Donne

MAN'S life is laid in the loom of time
To a pattern he does not see,
While the Weaver works and the shuttles fly
Till the doom of eternity.

Some shuttles are filled with silver thread,
And some with threads of gold;
While often but the darker hue
Is all that they may hold.

But the Weaver watches with skilful eye
Each shuttle fly to and fro,
And sees the pattern so deftly wrought
As the loom works slow and sure.

God surely planned that pattern,
Each thread – the dark and the fair –
Was chosen by his master skill
And placed in the web with care.

He only knows the beauty
And guides the shuttles which hold
The threads so unattractive
As well as the threads of gold.

Not till the loom is silent,
And the shuttles cease to fly
Shall God unroll the pattern
And explain the reason why.

The dark threads are as needful
In the Weaver's skilful hand
As the threads of gold and silver
In the pattern that he has planned.

J. Oswald Sanders

Our journey into God

Imperceptible as it may seem, each day we are developing as people and making progress on our journey into God.

HEAR my prayer, dear Lord;
do not stay silent when I weep;
for I am a foreigner here;
a pilgrim, like all my ancestors.
Overlook my guilt;
then I will take time to be happy,
before I leave this place
and cannot be found here any more.

Psalm 39:12–13

ALL these people died believing in, but having not yet received, the things that were promised them. They were like travellers seeing their destination far off, convinced about it, and glad of it, but openly admitting that they were foreigners and refugees here on earth. People who talk like that make it clear that they are on their way to their own country.

Hebrews 11:13–14

'FOR ever with the Lord!'
     Amen; so let it be:
Life from the dead is in that word,
'Tis immortality.
Here in the body pent,
Absent from thee I roam,
Yet nightly pitch my moving tent
A day's march nearer home.

James Montgomery

AT the start of your spiritual journey, you usually feel nothing but a kind of darkness all around your mind. We call this 'the cloud of unknowing'. It seems as if you know nothing and feel nothing except a longing for God in the depth of your being. However hard you try, this darkness, this cloud, blocks the way between you and your God. You will feel frustrated, because your mind cannot grasp God and your heart cannot enjoy God's love. Nevertheless, you can learn to feel at home in this darkness. Come back there as often as you can. Let your spirit call out to the one you love. If you hope, while still in this life, to see and feel God as he really is, it is only in this darkness and in this cloud that you will find him. If you try to love God, however, forgetting everything else, I am sure that God in his goodness will bring you to the point where you have deep experience of God himself. This is the journey of contemplation which I have urged you to begin.

The Cloud of Unknowing

GOD, my beloved, only love brings us close to you. Wherever you tread we are the earth under your foot.
Is it right that on the road of love
I should see the world in your company
but not see your face?

Mevlani Jalallud-din Rumi

FOR a soul to reach perfection, it usually has to pass through two important kinds of night. Teachers of mysticism call these experiences 'purgations' or 'purifications' of the soul; in this book I shall call them nights, for in both of them the soul travels as if by night, through the darkness. The first night consists of the purification of our senses; and the second is the purification of our spirit. . . .

The 'dark night of the senses' is the experience of beginners in prayer, when God begins to teach them how to contemplate him by shutting out all the distractions of the five senses. . . .

The 'dark night of the soul' is the experience of those who have already learnt how to pray, when God wants to bring them nearer to union with himself, by denying them even the feeling of his presence. . . .

There are three reasons why this journey made by the soul towards union with God is called 'night'. The first is because of the soul's point of departure: gradually the soul has to deprive itself of desire for all the worldly things which it possesses. Denying yourself all the things which pleased your senses is like going into the darkness of the night. The second reason is because of the route along which we must travel. The road is faith, which is only possible in the darkness when there is no certain knowledge. The third reason is because of the destination towards which we are travelling, which is union with God. God cannot be known by the senses or the intellect in this life, which is why we call it the dark night of the soul. These nights must pass through the soul – or, rather, the soul must pass through them – in order that it may arrive at divine union with God.

John of the Cross

ALL you have been, and seen, and done, and thought,
Not *you* but *I,* have seen, and been, and wrought:
I was the Sin which from Myself rebelled;
I the Remorse that toward Myself compelled;
I was the Tajidar who led the track:
I was the little Briar that pulled you back:
Sin and Contrition – Retribution owed,
And cancelled – Pilgrim, Pilgrimage, and Road,
Was but Myself toward Myself; and your
Arrival but *Myself* at my own door;
Who in your fraction of Myself behold
Myself within the mirror Myself hold
To see Myself in, and each part of Me
That sees himself, though drowned, shall ever see.
Come, you lost atoms, to your Centre draw,
And *be* the Eternal Mirror that you saw;
Rays that have wandered into darkness wide,
Return, and back into your Sun subside.

'Attar Farid ud-Din

ETERNAL Trinity! You are a deep sea. The deeper I go into this sea the more I find, and the more I find the more I want. You are the fire which burns without being consumed; you consume in your heat all the soul's self-love. You are the fire which melts all that is frigid. You are the light in whose light I can know all your truth. In the light of faith I am strong, constant and persevering. In the light of faith I hope – do not let me faint by the wayside. Truly this light is a sea; for the soul revels in you, eternal Trinity, like a child playing in the Sea of Peace. Clothe me, eternal truth, that I may run my race until the day I die, with true obedience and in the light of holy faith.

Catherine of Siena

THROUGH the day thy love has spared us;
    Now we lay us down to rest;
Through the silent watches guard us,
Let no foe our peace molest:
Jesus, thou our Guardian be;
Sweet it is to trust in thee.

Pilgrims here on earth, and strangers,
Dwelling in the midst of foes;
Us and ours preserve from dangers;
In thine arms may we repose,
And, when life's sad day is past,
Rest with thee in heaven at last.

Thomas Kelly

JESUS, our master, meet us while we walk in the way, and long to reach the heavenly country; so that, following your light we may keep the way of righteousness, and never wander away into the darkness of this world's night, while you, who are the Way, the Truth, and the

Life, are shining within us; for your own name's sake.
Amen.

The Mozarabic Sacramentary

L ORD Jesus,
   stay with us,
for evening is at hand and the day is past;
be our companion in the way,
kindle our hearts, and awaken hope,
that we may know you as you are revealed in Scripture
and the breaking of bread.
Grant this for the sake of your love. Amen.

The Roman Breviary of Paul VI

O Father, give me power to climb
   and wash in fountains filled with light,
weighed down no more by things of time,
lit by your shining in the night.
The sight of you begins our day,
with you its evening we shall spend;
you carry us, and lead the way,
the journey, and the journey's end.

Boethius

Farewell to the Soul of One Who Has Died

N., go forth upon your journey into God who created
you, in company with Jesus who died and came to life
again for you, and purified by the Holy Spirit of God who
has inspired you. As we let go of your visible presence, we
trust God to care for you, because God loves all that he
has made. Goodbye, N.; God be with you; farewell!

Adapted from the medieval prayer

Night Vigil

Some cannot sleep because they have work to do for the rest of us, or because they are in pain or anxiety.

'SENTRY, what news of the night?'
    someone called,
'Sentry, when will it end?'
'Morning is coming, but night will return,'
answered the sentry.
'If you really want to know, come again.'

Isaiah 21:11–12

Parents

Parents who are kept awake by caring for small children may begin to understand what is meant by saying that God our parent neither slumbers nor sleeps in his care for us. There is a long tradition of referring to God as both Father and Mother.

LORD, I am not proud,
    I keep my eyes cast down;
I have not concerned myself with great matters,
nor with things which are too hard for me;
Instead, I have settled down quietly,
like a child at its mother's breast,
like a child at its mother's breast.

Psalm 131:1–2

'WHEN Israel was a child, I loved him,'
      says God,
'out of Egypt I called my son.
The more I called them,
the further away from me they went;
my people sacrificed to Baal,
they offered incense to idols.
Yet I was the one who taught Israel to walk,
I gathered them up in my arms;
but they did not recognize
that it was I who cared for them.
I led them with cords of human kindness,
with ribbons of love.
I lifted them to my cheek,
as you would treat an infant;
I fed them tenderly like children.'

Hosea 11:1-4

SWEET and low, sweet and low,
   Wind of the western sea,
Low, low, breathe and blow,
Wind of the western sea,
Over the rolling waters go,
Come from the dying moon and blow,
Blow him again to me,
While my little one, while my pretty one sleeps.

Sleep and rest, sleep and rest,
Father will come to thee soon,
Rest, rest, on mother's breast.
Father will come to thee soon;
Father will come to his babe in the nest,
Silver sails all out of the west,
Under the silver moon,
Sleep my little one, sleep my pretty one, sleep.

Alfred, Lord Tennyson

THE chief priests and the religious experts were very angry, when they saw the amazing things Jesus had done in the Temple, and heard the children shouting, 'King from the royal family of David, save us now!'

'Do you hear what these children are shouting?' they spluttered.

'Yes,' answered Jesus. 'Have you never read where it says in the scriptures, "God has taught babies and toddlers to offer him perfect praise"?'

Matthew 21:15–16

SO I saw that God is glad to be our Father, and God is glad to be our Mother, and God is glad to be our true husband and to make our soul his beloved wife. . . .

So the Virgin Mary is our mother. We were all born of Mary's womb, for we are all 'in Christ'. That means that Mary, who is the Mother of our Saviour, is also the Mother of all down the ages who are saved by being 'in Christ'. But then Jesus our Saviour is also our true Mother, because day by day we are coming to new birth in Jesus. . . .

We know that when our earthly mothers gave us birth, we were born into a world of pain and death. But our true Mother, Jesus, who is all love, brings us into joy and eternal life. Praise to him! So he nourished us with love in his womb; then he was in labour with us; and when he came to full term, he suffered the sharpest agonies and the most terrible labour pains that anyone has ever endured or ever will; and at last he died. . . .

He could never die again, but he never stopped working; for after he had given us birth he had to feed us. The maternal instinct obliged him to care for us. An earthly mother lets her children suck her milk, but our precious Mother, Jesus, feeds us with himself. He feeds us, delicately and tenderly, with the Blessed Sacrament, which is the precious food of my life; in his mercy and grace he nourishes us with all the other sweet sacraments also. . . .

A kindly, loving mother who knows her child's needs cares for it tenderly; that is the nature of motherhood. As her child grows older, she changes her methods, but not her love. And when it is older still, she allows it to be beaten, in order to discourage vice, and to help the child grow in virtue and grace. This is the same method, fair and good, that our Lord uses with us: so he is like a Mother to us because he graciously disciplines us in small things in order to produce the higher virtues. . . .

Sometimes a mother may allow her children to fall down and hurt themselves, because they can learn from their mistakes. But she will never willingly allow her children to be in real danger, because she loves them. Occasionally an earthly mother cannot prevent the death of her child. Our heavenly Mother, Jesus, will not allow us his children to die, because he is almighty, all-wisdom and all-love. No one else is like that – glory to him!. . .

Often when we see how far we have fallen and how wretched we have become, we are so afraid and so greatly ashamed of ourselves, that we hardly know where to hide. But then our tender Mother does not wish us to run away, far from it. Rather, he wants us to do as children do; for when a child is hurt, or afraid, it quickly runs to its mother for help, as fast as it can. That is what he wants us to do, like a little child. He wants us to say, 'Kind Mother, gracious Mother, dear Mother, take pity on me: I have made myself filthy and displeasing to you. I cannot put it right without your help and grace.' And if we do not feel better immediately, be sure he behaves like a wise mother: if He sees that it is more use to us to cry for a while, he allows it, even though it distresses him, because he loves us so.

Julian of Norwich

JESUS, are you not a mother also? Are you not like a mother hen, who gathers her chicks under her wings? Really, Lord Jesus, you are a mother, and you understand those who are in labour. For by the pains of your death many souls have been born to life. Lord God, you are the great Mother. Both you and Jesus are mothers – mothers and fathers as well. Fathers by your authority, mothers by your kindness. Fathers by teaching, mothers by mercy. My soul, run under the wings of Jesus your mother, lament under his feathers. Ask for your wounds to be healed so that you may live again.

Anselm

The sick

As we remember in our prayers before we sleep those who cannot sleep because they are caring for children, so we should also pray for the sick and those who care for them.

AS we lie on our sick-bed,
Lord, put your arm around us,
hold us up and make us well.

Adapted from Psalm 41:3

THEY cry to the Lord in their distress;
he rescues them from their trouble;
he sends his word and heals them,
he saves them from the grave.

Psalm 107:19–20

ARE any of you sick? Then call the leaders of your congregation, and ask them to anoint you with oil in the name of the Lord and then pray for you. Prayer offered in faith will heal the sick person, and the Lord will lift them to their feet.

James 5:14–15

KEEP watch, dear Lord,
with those who wake or watch or weep tonight,
and give your angels charge over those who sleep.
Tend those who are sick, Lord Christ;
give rest to those who are weary;
bless those who are dying;
soothe those who are suffering;
pity those who are afflicted;
shield those who are joyous;
and all, for your love's sake. Amen.

Augustine of Hippo

AT even when the sun was set
The sick, O Lord, around thee lay;
O, in what divers pains they met!
O with what joy they went away!

Once more 'tis eventide, and we
Oppressed with various ills draw near;
What if thy form we cannot see?
We know and feel that thou art here.

O Saviour Christ, our woes dispel;
For some are sick, and some are sad,
And some have never loved thee well,
And some have lost the love they had;

And some have found the world is vain,
Yet from the world they break not free;
And some have friends who give them pain
Yet have not sought a friend in thee;

And none, O Lord, have perfect rest,
For none are wholly free from sin;
And they who fain would serve thee best
Are conscious most of wrong within.

O Saviour Christ, thou too art Man;
Thou hast been troubled, tempted, tried;
Thy kind but searching glance can scan
The very wounds that shame would hide;

Thy touch has still its ancient power,
No word from thee can fruitless fall;
Hear in this solemn evening hour,
And in thy mercy heal us all.

Henry Twells

For a Sick Child

THIS little one I hold is my child:
   she is your child also,
therefore be gracious to her.
She has come into a world of trouble;
sickness is in the world, and cold, and pain –
pain which you knew
and with which you were familiar.
Let her sleep peacefully,
for there is healing in sleep:
do not be angry with me or with my child.
Let her grow: let her become strong:
let her become full-grown:
then she will worship you and delight your heart.

From the Aro people, Sierra Leone

The troubled

Some cannot sleep because they are troubled in mind.

FROM the depths of despair I call out to you, Lord;
Lord, hear my cry;
listen to my call for help.

Psalm 130:1

JESUS our Friend, in your pity you took your disciples apart when they were weary because so many were coming and going; yet you knew what it was to spend a night in prayerful agony. Look in mercy on all whose sleep will be disturbed tonight, because they have work to do or are concerned for others, because they have unrepented sin or unresolved anger, or because they are alone and have not learnt to call you their friend. Forgive us and heal us, and grant your beloved ones sleep, for your love's sake. Amen.

Michael Counsell

THERE was a sudden storm, the wind blew and the waves were lapping into the boat, which was already filling up with water. Jesus was in the stern, sleeping in the head boatman's place. His disciples woke him up, crying, 'Rabbi! Don't you care that we're drowning?' When he woke up he gave the wind a telling off, and told the sea to be quiet. The wind stopped as suddenly as it began, and everything was completely calm. Jesus asked his disciples, 'Why were you so scared? How come you had no faith?' They were terrified, and started muttering to each other, 'Who is this? Even the wind and waves obey him!'

Mark 10:37–41

B UT (when so sad thou canst not sadder)
   Cry; – and upon thy so sore loss
Shall shine the traffic of Jacob's ladder
Pitched betwixt Heaven and Charing Cross.

Yea, in the night, my Soul, my daughter,
Cry, – clinging Heaven by the hems;
And lo, Christ walking on the water
Not of Gennesareth, but Thames!

Francis Thompson

R ISEN Christ, you came to your disciples in the
  evening on the first day of the week. Forgive us
when, like Thomas, we hug our doubts and worries to
ourselves. Grant us such a hunger for the fellowship of
those who believe in you, that no excuses may prevent us
from meeting together in the evening stillness. Then may
we find you standing among us, to strengthen us and send
us out in your service; for you are alive and reign, with the
Father and the Holy Spirit, one God now and for ever.
Amen.

Michael Counsell

Night workers

*Here is a prayer which includes those who have to work
at night – the police, fire and ambulance services, those
who maintain the public water, power and cleansing
services, and medical workers, among many others.*

R EMEMBER this night, O Lord, in your goodness:
  those who stand guard for us while we rest; those
who work to serve our needs on the morrow; those who

comfort the suffering and the bereaved; those who minister to and wait upon the dying. Grant that as we know their watching, so we may share their loving care; through Jesus Christ our Lord. Amen.

Massey Hamilton Shepherd, Jr

SCHOLARS take time to study if they want to be wise. It is the same with artists, and those who work night and day engraving precious stones, carefully working out new designs. They take great pains to produce a lifelike image, and will work far into the night to finish the work. It is the same with blacksmiths at their anvil, planning what they will make from a piece of iron. The heat from the fire sears their skin as they sweat away at the forge. The clanging of the hammer deafens them as they carefully watch the object they are working take shape. They take great pains to complete their task, and will work far into the night to bring it to perfection. It is the same with potters, sitting at their wheels and turning them with their feet, always concentrating on their work, concerned with how many objects they can produce. They work the clay with their feet until they can shape it with their hands: then they take great pains to glaze it properly, and will work far into the night to clean out the kiln.

All these people are skilled with their hands, each of them an expert at their own particular craft. Without such people there would be no cities; the work they do holds this world together. They pray about their work, and when they do their work, it is a form of prayer.

Ecclesiasticus (Sirach) 38:24, 27–32, 34

The unsleeping Church

It is comforting to remember that the Church of God offers up prayer and praise somewhere in the world twenty-four hours a day.

[IN the middle of the night the angel released Peter from prison.] After some thought, he decided to go to the house belonging to Mary, the mother of John Mark. Many people had gathered there to pray.

Acts 12:12

THE day thou gavest, Lord, is ended,
  the darkness falls at thy behest;
to thee our morning hymns ascended,
thy praise shall sanctify our rest.

We thank thee that thy Church unsleeping,
while earth rolls onward into light,
through all the world her watch is keeping,
and rests not now by day or night.

As o'er each continent and island
the dawn leads on another day,
the voice of prayer is never silent,
nor dies the strain of praise away.

The sun that bids us rest is waking
our brethren 'neath the western sky,
and hour by hour fresh lips are making
thy wondrous doings heard on high.

So be it, Lord; thy throne shall never,
like earth's proud empires, pass away;
thy kingdom stands, and grows for ever,
till all thy creatures own thy sway.

John Ellerton

Wakefulness

When we ourselves are unable to sleep, we can thank God for an opportunity for uninterrupted prayer.

IN the middle of the night I will get up to thank you because of your just decisions.

Psalm 119:62

I think about you, O God, while lying on my bed,
all night long I meditate;
it is as though my soul was enjoying a rich feast,
and I sing glad songs of praise
for you have been my help;
like a young bird nestling under its mother's wings
I shelter under your protection and sing for joy.

Psalm 63:5–7

JESUS went up into the hills to pray. He spent the whole night in prayer with God.

Luke 6:12

RECEIVE, O Lord, in heaven above
Our prayers and supplications pure;
Give us a heart all full of love
And steady courage to endure.

Thy holy name our mouths confess,
Our tongues are harps to praise thy grace;
Forgive our sins and wickedness,
Who in this vigil seek thy face.

Let not our song become a sigh,
A wail of anguish and despair;
In loving-kindness, Lord most high,
Receive tonight our evening prayer.

O raise us in that day, that we
May sing, where all thy Saints adore,
Praise to thy Father, and to thee,
And to thy Spirit, evermore.

Ephrem the Syrian

O Lord, the maker of all things,
we pray thee now in this evening hour,
to defend us through thy mercy
from all deceit of our enemy.
Let us not be deluded with dreams,
but if we lie awake keep thou our hearts.
Grant this petition, O Father,
to whom with the Holy Ghost,
always in heaven and earth,
be all laud, praise and honour. Amen.

Attributed to King Henry VIII

ABIDE with me; fast falls the eventide:
The darkness deepens; Lord, with me abide:
When other helpers fail, and comforts flee,
Help of the helpless, O abide with me.

Swift to its close ebbs out life's little day;
Earth's joys grow dim, its glories pass away;
Change and decay in all around I see:
O thou who changest not, abide with me.

I need thy presence every passing hour;
What but thy grace can foil the tempter's power?
Who like thyself my guide and stay can be?
Through cloud and sunshine, Lord, abide with me.

I fear no foe with thee at hand to bless;
Ills have no weight, and tears no bitterness.
Where is death's sting? Where, grave, thy victory?
I triumph still, if thou abide with me.

Hold thou thy Cross before my closing eyes;
Shine through the gloom, and point me to the skies:
Heaven's morning breaks, and earth's vain shadows flee;
In life, in death, O Lord, abide with me.

Henry Francis Lyte

GOD be in my head, and in my understanding;
God be in my eyes, and in my looking;
God be in my mouth, and in my speaking;
God be in my heart, and in my thinking;
God be at my end, and at my departing.

Pynson's Horae

ABIDE with us O Lord,
until the Day-Star ariseth,
and the Morning Light appeareth,
when we shall abide with thee, for ever. Amen.

James Burns

From 'St Patrick's Breastplate'

CHRIST be with me, Christ within me,
   Christ behind me, Christ before me,
Christ beside me, Christ to win me,
Christ to comfort and restore me,
Christ beneath me, Christ above me,
Christ in quiet, Christ in danger,
Christ in hearts of all that love me,
Christ in mouth of friend and stranger.

God With Me Lying Down

GOD with me lying down,
   God with me rising up,
God with me in each ray of light,
Nor I a ray of joy without Him,
   Nor one ray without Him.

Christ with me sleeping,
Christ with me waking,
Christ with me watching,
Every day and night,
   Each day and night.

God with me protecting,
The Lord with me directing,
The Spirit with me strengthening,
For ever and for evermore,
   Ever and evermore, Amen.
      Chief of chiefs, Amen.

                Carmina Gadelica I, 5

Repose of Sleep

O God of life, darken not to me Thy light,
O God of life, close not to me Thy joy,
O God of life, shut not to me Thy door,
O God of life, refuse not to me Thy mercy,
O God of life, quench Thou to me Thy wrath,
And O God of life, crown Thou to me Thy gladness,
O God of life, crown Thou to me Thy gladness.

Carmina Gadelica III, 343

I Lie Down This Night

I lie down this night with God,
And God will lie down with me;
I lie down this night with Christ,
And Christ will lie down with me;
I lie down this night with Spirit,
And the Spirit will lie down with me;
God and Christ and the Spirit
Be lying down with me.

Carmina Gadelica III, 333

SUN of my soul, thou Saviour dear,
It is not night if thou be near.
O may no earth-born cloud arise
To hide thee from thy servant's eyes.

When the soft dews of kindly sleep
My wearied eyelids gently steep,
Be my last thought, how sweet to rest
For ever on my Saviour's breast.

Abide with me from morn till eve,
For without thee I cannot live;
Abide with me when night is nigh,
For without thee I dare not die.

If some poor wand'ring child of thine
Have spurned to-day the voice divine,
Now, Lord, the gracious work begin;
Let him no more lie down in sin.

Watch by the sick; enrich the poor
With blessings from thy boundless store;
Be every mourner's sleep to-night
Like infant's slumbers, pure and light.

Come near and bless us when we wake,
Ere through the world our way we take;
Till in the ocean of thy love
We lose ourselves in heaven above.

John Keble

A T night you lay within the boat, asleep:
   Then woke, and gave commands to wind and sea.
O Christ, although my body slumbers deep,
Still may my heart keep patient watch with thee.
O Lamb of God, our souls in safety keep;
Protect us now against our enemy.

Alcuin of York

N O W from the altar of my heart
   Let incense flames arise;
Assist me, Lord, to offer up
Mine evening sacrifice.

Minutes and mercies multiplied
Have made up all this day;
Minutes came quick, but mercies were
More fleet and free than they.

New time, new favour, and new joys
Do a new song require;
Till I shall praise thee as I would,
Accept my heart's desire.

John Mason

O most loving Father, who willest us to give thanks for all things, to dread nothing but the loss of thee, and to cast all our care on thee, who carest for us; preserve us from faithless fears and worldly anxieties, and grant that no clouds of this mortal life may hide us from the light of that Love which is immortal, and which thou hast manifested unto us in thy Son Jesus Christ our Lord. Amen.

William Bright

God in the silence

In the silence and the darkness many have had a new sense of the presence, the mystery and the depths of God.

AWE before God will stop you from sinning; silently meditate as you lie on your bed and be still.

Psalm 4:4

THE angel of the Lord came to Elijah a second time and touched him, saying, 'Get up and eat, or the journey will be too much for you.' So he got up, ate and drank, and that food gave him enough strength to travel for forty days and forty nights to Horeb, the Mountain of God. There he found a cave, and spent the night there. Suddenly, a message from the Lord came to him. He heard a voice saying . . . 'Go out and stand on the mountain before the Lord; you will know when the Lord passes by.' There followed a great, strong wind, tearing the mountain and breaking the rocks in pieces before the Lord – but the Lord was not in the wind. And after the wind an earthquake – but the Lord was not in the earthquake. And after the earthquake a fire – but the Lord was not in the fire. And after the fire – the sound of utter silence.

So – when Elijah became aware of it, he wrapped his cloak over his face; he went out, and stood at the mouth of the cave. All at once, he heard a voice, which asked him, 'What are you doing here, Elijah?'

1 Kings 19:7–9, 11–13

R OUND me falls the night;
   Saviour, be my Light:
Through the hours in darkness shrouded
Let me see thy face unclouded;
Let thy glory shine
In this heart of mine.

Earthly work is done,
Earthly sounds are none;
Rest in sleep and silence seeking,
Let me hear thee softly speaking;
In my spirit's ear
Whisper, 'I am near.'

Blessed, heavenly Light,
Shining through earth's night;
Voice, that oft of love hast told me;
Arms, so strong to clasp and hold me;
Thou thy watch wilt keep,
Saviour, o'er my sleep.

William Romanis

ABIDE with us, O most blessed and merciful Saviour, for it is toward evening and the day is far spent. As long as thou art present with us, we are in the light. When thou art present all is brightness, all is sweetness. We discourse with thee, watch with thee, live with thee and lie down with thee. Abide then with us, O thou whom our soul loveth, thou Sun of righteousness with healing under thy wings arise in our hearts; make thy light then to shine in darkness as a perfect day in the dead of night.

Henry Vaughan

BE still in God's presence,
    be still in God's presence,
be still in God's presence,
    and love and be loved.

Be still in God's presence,
    be still in God's presence,
be still in God's presence,
    and love and be loved.

Fall deep in the silence,
    fall deep in the silence,
fall deep in the silence,
    the silence of God.

Fall deep in the silence,
    fall deep in the silence,
fall deep in the silence,
    the silence of God.

Jim Cotter
(may be sung to the tune of 'The Ash Grove')

GOD of love,
whose Son Jesus Christ spent whole nights
in prayer with you:
if we wake in the silence,
help us to be still and know that you are God.
If we have thoughts to share with you,
give us confidence to do so,
knowing that you completely understand;
but if no words come to our minds,
may your Holy Spirit use the space within our hearts
to pray with yearnings too deep to be uttered;
for you, O blessed Trinity,
live and reign in the stillness of perfect love,
one God for ever and ever. Amen.

Michael Counsell

Troubles and worries

*If we lie awake because of worries and doubts, we can
remember that it is not we who are searching for God,
but God who is searching for us.*

LORD God, my Saviour, I have cried in the day,
and in the night before you.
Hear my prayer; listen to my cry for help!
My life is full of trouble, and I am near to death.

Psalm 88:1–3

LET the words of my mouth
and the meditations of my heart
be pleasing in your sight,
O Lord, my Rock and my Redeemer.

Psalm 19:14

ONCE as they were travelling, Jesus went into one of the villages, and a woman called Martha let him stay in her house. She had a sister called Mary, who spent her time sitting near to Jesus, listening to him. Martha, however, was going crazy with all the things she had to do to get the meal ready.

'Sir,' she protested, coming up to him, 'don't you care that this sister of mine has left me to do everything? Tell her she's got to help me!'

'Martha, Martha,' said Jesus, 'You are worried and troubled about so many things! There's only one thing you really need. Mary has chosen the right way, and she will never lose it.'

Luke 10:38–42

GRANT calmness and control of thought to those who are facing uncertainty and anxiety: let their heart stand fast, believing in the Lord. Be all things to all men, knowing each one and their petition, each house and its need, for the sake of Jesus Christ. Amen.

Russian Orthodox

O God, the Father everlasting, who in thy wondrous grace, standest within the shadows, keeping watch over thine own; grant that in every peril and perplexity, in our groping and weariness, we may know the comfort of thy pervading presence. When the day grows dark may we fear no evil because thy hand is upon us. Lead us onwards through the darkness into thy light, through the sorrows into the joy of the Lord, and through the cross of sacrifice into closer communion with thy Son, even Jesus Christ our Lord. Amen.

J. Hunter

The Hound of Heaven

I fled Him, down the nights and down the days;
  I fled Him, down the arches of the years;
I fled Him, down the labyrinthine ways
  Of my own mind; and in the mist of tears
I hid from Him, and under running laughter.
    Up vistaed hopes I sped;
    And shot, precipitated,
Adown Titanic glooms of chasmed fears,
  From those strong Feet that followed, followed after.
    But with unhurrying chase,
    And unperturbèd pace,
  Deliberate speed, majestic instancy,
    They beat – and a Voice beat
    More instant than the Feet –
'All things betray thee, who betrayest Me.'

    I pleaded, outlaw-wise,
By many a hearted casement, curtained red,
  Trellised with intertwining charities;
(For, though I knew His love Who followèd,
    Yet was I sore adread
Lest, having Him, I must have naught beside)
But, if one little casement parted wide,
  The gust of His approach would clash it to:
  Fear wist not to evade, as Love wist to pursue.
Across the margent of the world I fled,
  And troubled the gold gateways of the stars,
  Smiting for shelter on their clangèd bars;
    Fretted to dulcet jars
And silvern chatter the pale ports o' the moon.
I said to Dawn: Be sudden – to Eve: Be soon;
  With thy young skiey blossoms heap me over
    From this tremendous Lover –

Float thy vague veil about me, lest He see!
    I tempted all His servitors, but to find
My own betrayal in their constancy,

In faith to Him their fickleness to me,
    Their traitorous trueness, and their loyal deceit.
To all swift things for swiftness did I sue;
    Clung to the whistling mane of every wind.
        But whether they swept, smoothly fleet,
    The long savannahs of the blue;
        Or whether, Thunder-driven,
        They clanged his chariot 'thwart a heaven,
Plashy with flying lightnings round the spurn o' their feet:
    Fear wist not to evade as Love wist to pursue.
        Still with unhurrying chase,
        And unperturbèd pace,
    Deliberate speed, majestic instancy,
        Came on the following Feet,
        And a Voice above their beat –
'Naught shelters thee, who wilt not shelter Me.'

I sought no more that after which I strayed
        In face of man or maid;
But still within the little children's eyes
        Seems something, something that replies,
They at least are for me, surely for me!
I turned me to them very wistfully;
But just as their young eyes grew sudden fair
        With dawning answers there,
Their angel plucked them from me by the hair.
'Come then, ye other children, Nature's – share
With me' (said I) 'your delicate fellowship;
    Let me greet you lip to lip,
    Let me twine with you caresses,
        Wantoning

130

With our Lady-Mother's vagrant tresses,
    Banqueting
With her in her wind-walled palace,
Underneath her azured daïs,
Quaffing, as your taintless way is,
    From a chalice
Lucent-weeping out of the dayspring.'
    So it was done:
I in their delicate fellowship was one –
Drew the bolt of Nature's secrecies.
    I knew all the swift importings
    On the wilful face of skies;
    I knew how the clouds arise
    Spumèd of the wild sea-snortings;
        All that's born or dies
    Rose and drooped with; made them shapers
Of mine own moods, or wailful or divine;
    With them joyed and was bereaven.
    I was heavy with the even,
    When she lit her glimmering tapers
    Round the day's dead sanctities.
    I laughed in the morning's eyes.
I triumphed and I saddened with all weather,
    Heaven and I wept together,
And its sweet tears were salt with mortal mine;
Against the red throb of its sunset-heart
    I laid my own to beat,
    And share commingling heat;
But not by that, by that, was eased my human smart.
In vain my tears were wet on Heaven's grey cheek.
For ah! we know not what each other says,
    These things and I; in sound *I* speak –
Their sound is but their stir, they speak by silences.
Nature, poor stepdame, cannot slake my drouth;
    Let her, if she would owe me,

Drop yon blue bosom-veil of sky, and show me
    The breasts o' her tenderness:
Never did any milk of hers once bless
    My thirsting mouth.
    Nigh and nigh draws the chase,
    With unperturbèd pace,
  Deliberate speed, majestic instancy;
    And past those noisèd Feet
    A Voice comes yet more fleet
  'Lo! naught contents thee, who content'st not Me.'

Naked I wait Thy love's uplifted stroke!
My harness piece by piece Thou hast hewn from me,
    And smitten me to my knee;
    I am defenceless utterly.
    I slept, methinks, and woke,
And, slowly gazing, find me stripped in sleep.
In the rash lustihead of my young powers,
    I shook the pillaring hours
And pulled my life upon me; grimed with smears,
I stand amid the dust o' the mounded years –
My mangled youth lies dead beneath the heap.
My days have crackled and gone up in smoke,
Have puffed and burst as sun-starts on a stream.
    Yea, faileth now even dream
The dreamer, and the lute the lutanist;
Even the linked fantasies, in whose blossomy twist
I swung the earth a trinket at my wrist,
Are yielding; cords of all too weak account
For earth with heavy griefs so overplussed.
    Ah! is Thy love indeed
A weed, albeit an amaranthine weed,
Suffering no flowers except its own to mount?
    Ah! must –
    Designer infinite!

Ah! must Thou char the wood ere Thou canst limn with
    it?
My freshness spent its wavering shower i' the dust;
And now my heart is as a broken fount,
Wherein tear-drippings stagnate, spilt down ever
      From the dank thoughts that shiver
Upon the sighful branches of my mind.
      Such is; what is to be?
The pulp so bitter, how shall taste the rind?
I dimly guess what Time in mists confounds;
Yet ever and anon a trumpet sounds
From the hid battlements of Eternity;
Those shaken mists a space unsettle, then
Round the half-glimpsed turrets slowly wash again.
      But not ere him who summoneth
      I first have seen, enwound
With glooming robes purpureal, cypress-crowned;
His name I know, and what his trumpet saith.
Whether man's heart or life it be which yields
      Thee harvest, must Thy harvest-fields
      Be dunged with rotten death?
      Now of that long pursuit
      Comes on at hand the bruit;
   That Voice is round me like a bursting sea:
    'And is thy earth so marred,
    Shattered in shard on shard?
   Lo, all things fly thee, for thou fliest Me!
      Strange, piteous, futile thing!
Wherefore should any set thee love apart?
Seeing none but I makes much of naught' (He said),
'And human love needs human meriting:
      How hast thou merited
Of all man's clotted clay the dingiest clot?
    Alack, thou knowest not
How little worthy of any love thou art!

Whom wilt thou find to love ignoble thee,
    Save Me, save only Me?
All which I took from thee I did but take,
    Not for thy harms,
But just that thou might'st seek it in My arms.
    All which thy child's mistake
Fancies as lost, I have stored for thee at home:
    Rise, clasp My hand, and come!'

    Halts by me that footfall:
    Is my gloom, after all,
Shade of His hand, outstretched caressingly?
    'Ah, fondest, blindest, weakest,
    I am He Whom thou seekest!
Thou dravest love from thee, who dravest Me.'

Francis Thompson

The Sorrow Tree

THE Hasidim were members of a mystical Jewish movement in Russia a couple of centuries ago. When they were arguing about who had suffered the most, their spiritual leader told them a story. On Judgement Day, he said, everyone will be allowed to hang up all their own personal miseries on one of the branches of the huge Tree of Sorrows. Then they will all walk round the tree, looking for someone else's burdens, which they would rather carry than their own. In the end, he said, every person will take back their own sorrows, because they seem more bearable than any of the others.

Traditional

Pain

Is it our own pain which keeps us awake? God does not want his children to suffer, but many Christians have found lessons to be learnt from their illnesses.

I cry aloud to God;
   I cry out, and God listens to me;
when I am in pain I pray to the Lord;
all night long I lift up my hands in prayer;
but I cannot find comfort anywhere.

Psalm 77:1–2

SO that I should not become proud, I was given a thorn in my flesh, a secret agent of Satan which he sent to beat me up and humiliate me. Three times I begged the Lord to take it away. God replied, 'My gracious love is all you need. My power will be recognized most clearly when I work through weak people.'

2 Corinthians 12:7–9

Hymn to God My God, in My Sickness

SINCE I am coming to that holy room,
   Where, with thy choir of saints for evermore,
I shall be made thy music; as I come
I tune the instrument here at the door,
And what I must do then, think here before.

Whilst my physicians by their love are grown
Cosmographers, and I their map, who lie
Flat on this bed, that by them may be shown
That this is my south-west discovery
Per fretum febris, by these straits to die.

I joy, that in these straits, I see my west;
For, though their currents yield return to none,
What shall my west hurt me? As west and east
In all flat maps (and I am one) are one,
So death doth touch the resurrection.

Is the Pacific Sea my home? Or are
The eastern riches? Is Jerusalem?
Anyan, and Magellan, and Gibraltar,
All straits, and none but straits, are ways to them,
Whether where Japhet dwelt, or Cham, or Shem.

We think that Paradise and Calvary,
Christ's Cross, and Adam's tree, stood in one place;
Look Lord, and find both Adams met in me;
As the first Adam's sweat surrounds my face,
May the last Adam's blood my soul embrace.

So, in his purple wrapped receive me Lord,
By these his thorns give me his other crown;
And as to others' souls I preached thy word,
Be this my text, my sermon to mine own,
Therefore that he may raise the Lord throws down.

John Donne

O Love that will not let me go,
    I rest my weary soul in Thee:
I give Thee back the life I owe,
That in Thine ocean depth its flow
May richer, fuller be.

O Light that followest all my way,
I yield my flickering torch to Thee:
My heart restores its borrowed ray,
That in Thy sunshine's blaze its day
May brighter, fairer be.

O Joy that seekest me through pain,
I cannot close my heart to Thee:
I trace the rainbow through the rain,
And feel the promise is not vain
That morn shall tearless be.

O Cross that liftest up my head,
I dare not ask to fly from Thee:
I lay in dust life's glory dead,
And from the ground there blossoms red
Life that shall endless be.

George Matheson

CALL the world if you please 'The Vale of Soul-making'. Then you will find out the use of the world. . . . I will call the world a school instituted for the purpose of teaching little children to read. I will call the human heart the horn-book read in that school. And I will call the child able to read, the soul made from that school and its horn-book. Do you not see how necessary a world of pains and troubles is to school an intelligence and make it a soul?

John Keats

Light in the darkness

It must have been the sense of God's presence in the night that has led many writers to describe God as light.

YOU, Lord, will light my candle:
the Lord my God turns my darkness into light.
With you is the fountain of life,
and in your light we shall see light.
Dear God, bring us back to you again,
make your presence our light, and we shall be saved.

Psalms 18:28; 36:9; 80:3

O God, I fear thee not because
   I dread the wrath to come: for how
Can such affright, when never was
A friend more excellent than thou?
Thou knowest well the heart's design,
The secret purpose of the mind,
And I adore thee, light divine,
Lest lesser lights should make me blind.

Abu-l-Husain al-Nuri

God Knows

I said to the man who stood at the gate of the year: 'Give
   me a light that I may tread safely into the unknown.'
   And he replied: 'Go out into the darkness and put your
hand into the hand of God. That shall be to you better
than light and safer than a known way.'
   So I went forth, and finding the Hand of God, trod
gladly into the night. And he led me towards the hills and
the breaking of day in the lone East.

So heart be still:
What need our little life
Our human life to know,
   If God hath comprehension?
In all the dizzy strife
Of things both high and low,
   God hideth his intention.

God knows. His will
Is best. The stretch of years
Which wind ahead, so dim
   To our imperfect vision,
Are clear to God. Our fears

Are premature: in him
 All time hath full provision.

 Then rest; until
God moves to lift the veil
From our impatient eyes,
 When, as the sweet features
Of life's stern face we hail,
Far beyond all surmise
 God's thought around his creatures
  Our mind shall fill.

Minnie Louise Haskins

HOLY Father, cheer our way
 With thy love's perpetual ray;
Grant us every closing day
Light at evening time.

Holy Saviour, calm our fears
When earth's brightness disappears;
Grant us in our latter years
Light at evening time.

Holy Spirit, be thou nigh
When in mortal pains we lie;
Grant us, as we come to die,
Light at evening time.

Holy, blessed Trinity,
Darkness is not dark with thee;
Those thou keepest always see
Light at evening time.

Richard Hayes Robinson

O Lord God, who art light eternal,
in the brightness of whose countenance
is day that knows no night,
and in thy protecting arms all quietness and tranquillity.
While the darkness covers the face of the earth,
receive our body and soul unto thy care and keeping;
that whether we sleep or wake,
we may rest in thee,
in thy light beholding light;
through Jesus Christ our Lord. Amen.

Jeremy Taylor

THE Lord is my light and my salvation;
whom then need I fear?
The Lord is the strength of my life;
of whom need I be afraid?

Psalm 27:1

DISPEL, O Lord, O Father of lights,
all clouds of doubt,
and the darkness about our earthly course,
that in thy light we may see light,
and come both to know thee as we are known,
and to love as we are loved;
through Jesus Christ our Lord. Amen.

John Donne

LORD God, enlighten the blindness of our minds with
the knowledge of the truth: that in thy light we may
see light, and, at the last, in the light of grace, the light of
glory; through Jesus Christ our Lord. Amen.

Lancelot Andrewes

IF I say, 'Surely, the darkness will hide me,'
even the night will become light around me;
for darkness is not darkness to you,
but the night shines as bright as the day;
the darkness and light are both alike to you.

Psalm 139:11–12

GOD of hope, the true light of faithful souls and
perfect brightness of the blessed, you are indeed the
light of the world; grant that our hearts may both render
you a worthy prayer, and always glorify you with the
offering of praises, through Jesus Christ our Lord. Amen.

The Gelasian Sacramentary

INCLINE, O Lord, your merciful ears, and illumine
the darkness of our hearts by the light of your visita-
tion; through Jesus Christ our Lord. Amen.

The Gelasian Sacramentary

O God, with whom is the well of life, and in whose
light we see light, increase in us, we pray, the brightness of divine knowledge, whereby we may be able to
reach your plenteous fountain; impart to our thirsting
souls the draught of life, and restore to our darkened
minds the light from Heaven; through Jesus Christ our
Lord. Amen.

The Mozarabic Breviary

ALMIGHTY and everlasting God, at evening, and
morning, and noonday, we humbly ask you to drive
from our hearts the darkness of sin, and make us to come
to the true light, which is Christ; through the same Jesus
Christ your Son. Amen.

The Gelasian Sacramentary

L ORD Jesus, you are light from light eternal.
   You have illuminated all spiritual darkness;
my soul is filled by your brightness.
Your light gives beauty to all things;
you light up the skies with the sun and the moon,
and ordered night and day to succeed each other in peace;
so you made the sun and the moon to be friends:
may I be friends with all those I meet.
At night you give us rest for our bodies;
by day you give us strength to work.
Help me to work diligently and with devotion,
so that at night my conscience may be at peace.
As I lie down on my bed at night,
your fingers will close my eyelids:
lay your hand on my head to bless me,
so that the sleep of the just may be mine.

Gregory of Nazianzus

L EAD, kindly light, amid the encircling gloom,
   Lead thou me on;
The night is dark, and I am far from home;
   Lead thou me on.
Keep thou my feet; I do not ask to see
The distant scene: one step enough for me.

I was not ever thus, nor prayed that thou
   Shouldst lead me on;
I loved to choose and see my path; but now
   Lead thou me on.
I loved the garish day, and, spite of fears,
Pride ruled my will: remember not past years.

So long thy power hath blest me, sure it still
　　Will lead me on
O'er moor and fen, o'er crag and torrent, till
　　The night is gone,
And with the morn those angel faces smile
Which I have loved long since, and lost awhile.

John Henry Newman

O Lord God almighty, as you have taught us to call the evening, the morning and the noonday one day; and have made the sun to know its going down; dispel the darkness of our hearts, that by your brightness we may know you to be the true God and eternal light, living and reigning for ever and ever. Amen.

The Mozarabic Breviary

GRANT us your light, O Lord:
　　that the darkness of our hearts being done away,
we may come to the true light,
even Christ our Saviour. Amen.

The Sarum Breviary

Angels and the Communion of Saints

We are never alone, even when no earthly people are with us, for the whole company of heaven is always and everywhere invisibly present.

A T sunset Jacob found a place and spent the night there. He chose some stones for a pillow and lay down. He dreamt that he could see a ladder reaching from earth to heaven, with the angels of God going up and down on it.

Then he saw the Lord standing at the top of the ladder. 'I am the Lord, the God of your ancestors Abraham and Isaac,' he said. 'I will give to you and your descendants the land which you are now lying on. Your descendants will be as numerous as the grains of dust on the earth. They will spread out to north, east, south and west, and all the families on earth will be grateful for you and your descendants. I promise to protect you in every place to which you go, and then bring you back to this land. You can be sure that I will be with you until I have done what I have promised.'

When Jacob woke up, he thought, 'To be sure, the Lord is in this place, and I did not know.' He was frightened, and said to himself, 'This is an amazing place! This can only be the house of God, and the gateway to heaven.'

Genesis 28:11–17

S O we too should be persistent in running the race which we have been entered for, since we are surrounded by so great a cloud of spectators. We should strip off our selfish habits and anything else which encumbers and hinders us, and look at Jesus, who stands at the starting line and the finishing tape of the race of faith. To win the prize of joy, he put up with the agony of the cross, paying no attention to the disgrace of it. Now he is in the winner's seat, at the right-hand side of God's throne.

Hebrews 12:1–2

I Lie In My Bed

I lie in my bed
    As I would lie in the grave,
Thine arm beneath my neck,
    Thou Son of Mary victorious.

Angels shall watch me
And I lying in slumber,
And angels shall guard me
    In the sleep of the grave.

Uiriel shall be at my feet,
Ariel shall be at my back,
Gabriel shall be at my head,
    And Raphael shall be at my side.

Michael shall be with my soul,
The strong shield of my love!
And the Physician Son of Mary
Shall put the salve to mine eye,
    The Physician Son of Mary
    Shall put the salve to mine eye!

Carmina Gadelica I, 95

THE Angels of God guard us through the night
and quieten the powers of darkness.
The Spirit of God be our guide
to lead us to peace and glory.

Jim Cotter

A story is told of a medieval monastery where the
monks worked very hard to make their singing as
beautiful as possible. But there was one old monk who
had a voice like a corn-crake, and nothing they could do
would make him sing in tune. Then one night they looked
up and saw that the rafters were filled with angels listening attentively to their worship. 'What an honour,' cried
the abbot. 'The angels have made themselves visible
because they are impressed by the quality of our singing.
We shall have to send our brother to a neighbouring
monastery so that he does not spoil it.' So he was
despatched without delay, but the next night it was found
that all the angels had followed him to the other
monastery: it was not the quality of the singing, but the
beauty of his silent prayers, that they were listening to.

Anonymous

CHRIST walk with me on every way
and where I live, no harm be done;
the Trinity be where I stay:
Father, Holy Spirit, Son.
Bright angels smooth the paths I tread
that men and women walk them free;
your Word be in each word that's said,
and children run to welcome me.

Ascribed to St Columba

LORD, keep us safe this night,
Secure from all our fears;
May angels guard us while we sleep,
Till morning light appears.

John Leland

IN this life and beyond,
with our ancestors of the flesh,
in company with the Saints,
in love for those we have known,
all glory and praise to God.

Jim Cotter

AND now another day is gone,
I'll sing my Maker's praise,
My comforts every hour make known,
His providence and grace.

I lay my body down to sleep;
May angels guard my head,
And through the hours of darkness keep
Their watch around my bed.

With cheerful heart I close my eyes,
Since thou wilt not remove;
And in the morning let me rise
Rejoicing in thy love.

Isaac Watts

BUT when we consider with a religious seriousness the
manifold weakness of the strongest devotions in time
of prayer, it is a sad consideration. I throw myself down in
my chamber, and I call in and invite God and his angels
thither, and when they are there, I neglect God and his

angels for the noise of a fly, for the rattling of a coach, for the whining of a door; I talk on, in the same posture of praying, eyes lifted up, knees bowed down, as though I prayed to God; and if God or his angels should ask me when I thought last of God in that prayer, I cannot tell: sometimes I find that I had forgot what I was about, but when I began to forget it, I cannot tell. A memory of yesterday's pleasures, a fear of tomorrow's dangers, a straw under my knee, a noise in mine ear, a light in mine eye, an anything, a nothing, a fancy, a chimera in my brain troubles me in my prayer. So certainly there is nothing, nothing in spiritual things, perfect in this world.

John Donne

THE radiant morn hath passed away,
  And spent too soon her golden store;
The shadows of departing day
Creep on once more.

Our life is but an autumn sun,
Its glorious noon how quickly past;
Lead us, O Christ, our life-work done,
Safe home at last.

O by thy soul-inspiring grace
Uplift our hearts to realms on high;
Help us to look to that bright place
Beyond the sky,

Where light, and life, and joy, and peace
In undivided empire reign,
And thronging angels never cease
Their deathless strain;

Where saints are clothed in spotless white,
And evening shadows never fall,
Where thou, eternal Light of light,
Art Lord of all.

Godfrey Thring

WHERE is heaven? Is it some millions of leagues from us, far beyond the sun and the fixed stars? What have immortal spirits to do with space and place? Who knows, but a heaven-born soul, who is freed from the clog of this vile body, and filled with all the fullness of God, may pass as easily and quickly from one verge of the creation to the other, as our thoughts can change and fly from east to west, from the past to the future? Perhaps, even now, we live in the midst of this glorious assembly; heaven is there where our God and Saviour displays himself; and do not you feel him near you, nearer than any of his visible works? Perhaps there is nothing but this thin partition of flesh and blood between us and those blessed spirits that are before the throne. If our eyes were open, we should see the mountains around us covered with chariots and horses of fire; if our ears were unstopped we should hear the praises of our great Immanuel resounding in the air, as once the shepherds heard. What a comfortable meditation is this to strengthen our weak faith in such a dark declining day as this, when sense would almost persuade us that we are left to serve God alone!

John Newton

THEY lack not friends that have thy love,
    And may converse and walk with thee,
And with thy saints here and above,
With whom for ever I must be.

In the blest fellowship of saints
Is wisdom, safety and delight;
And when my heart declines and faints,
It's raisèd by their heat and light.

As for my friends, they are not lost:
The several vessels of thy fleet,
Though parted now, by tempests tossed,
Shall safely in the haven meet.

Still we are centred all in thee,
Members, though distant, of one Head;
In the same family we be,
By the same faith and spirit led.

Before thy throne we daily meet
As joint-petitioners to thee;
In spirit we each other greet,
And shall again each other see.

The heavenly hosts, world without end,
Shall be my company above;
And thou, my best and surest friend,
Who shall divide me from thy love?

            Richard Baxter (first line altered)

GOD'S saints are shining lights; who stays
       Here long must pass
O'er dark hills, swift streams and steep ways
       As smooth as glass:
But these all night,
Like candles, shed
Their beams and light
Us into bed.
They are – indeed – our pillar fires
Seen as we go;
They are that city's shining spires
We travel to.

Henry Vaughan

HARK! hark, my soul! Angelic songs are swelling
       O'er earth's green fields, and ocean's wave-beat
   shore;
How sweet the truth those blessèd strains are telling
       Of that new life when sin shall be no more!
Angels of Jesus, angels of light,
Singing to welcome the pilgrims of the night!

Onward we go, for still we hear them singing:
       'Come, weary souls, for Jesus bids you come';
And through the dark, its echoes sweetly ringing,
       The music of the Gospel leads us home.
Angels of Jesus, angels of light,
Singing to welcome the pilgrims of the night!

Far, far away, like bells at evening pealing,
       The voice of Jesus sounds o'er land and sea,
And laden souls, by thousands meekly stealing,
       Kind Shepherd, turn their weary steps to thee.
Angels of Jesus, angels of light,
Singing to welcome the pilgrims of the night!

Rest comes at length; though life be long and dreary,
    The day must dawn, and darksome night be past;
All journeys end in welcomes to the weary,
    And heaven, the heart's true home, will come at last.
Angels of Jesus, angels of light,
Singing to welcome the pilgrims of the night!

Angels! sing on, your faithful watches keeping,
    Sing us sweet fragments of the songs above;
While we toil on, and soothe ourselves with weeping,
    Till life's long night shall break in endless love.
Angels of Jesus, angels of light,
Singing to welcome the pilgrims of the night!

Frederick William Faber

GOD, that madest earth and heaven,
    Darkness and light,
Who the day for toil hast given,
For rest the night;
May thine angel-guards defend us,
Slumber sweet thy mercy send us,
Holy dreams and hopes attend us,
This livelong night.

Reginald Heber

MAY your angels, holy Son,
    Guard our homes when day is done,
When at peace, our sleep is best:
Bid them watch us while we rest.

Prince of everything that is,
High Priest of the mysteries,
Let your angels, God supreme,
Tell us truth dressed as a dream.

May no terror and no fright
Spoil our slumber in the night;
Free from care our eyelids close;
Spirit, give us prompt repose.

We have laboured through the day:
Lift our burdens when we pray,
Then our souls in safety keep,
That our sleep be soft and deep.

Attributed to St Patrick

FOR all the Saints who from their labours rest,
Who thee by faith before the world confest,
Thy name, O Jesu, be for ever blest.
    Alleluia!

Thou wast their Rock, their Fortress, and their Might;
Thou Lord, their Captain in the well-fought fight;
Thou in the darkness drear their one true Light.
    Alleluia!

O may thy soldiers, faithful, true, and bold,
Fight as the Saints who nobly fought of old,
And win, with them, the victor's crown of gold.
    Alleluia!

O blest communion, fellowship divine!
We feebly struggle, they in glory shine;
Yet all are one in thee, for all are thine.
    Alleluia!

And when the strife is fierce, the warfare long,
Steals on the ear the distant triumph-song,
And hearts are brave again, and arms are strong.
    Alleluia!

The golden evening brightens in the west;
Soon, soon to faithful warriors cometh rest:
Sweet is the calm of Paradise the blest.
  Alleluia!

But lo! there breaks a yet more glorious day;
The Saints triumphant rise in bright array:
The King of glory passes on his way.
  Alleluia!

From earth's wide bounds, from ocean's farthest coast,
Through gates of pearl streams in the countless host,
Singing to Father, Son, and Holy Ghost,
  Alleluia!

William Walsham How

The Stars

As many poets have sung, we gain a new insight into the beauty of God's creation when we see the sky at night.

THE sky was made when God spoke,
and as soon as the words were out of his mouth
there was an army of stars.
God made the two great lights:
the great one to be in charge of the day,
and the smaller one with the stars to look after the night.
When the foundations of the earth were dug,
and its cornerstone was laid,
then all the morning stars sang together,
and the sons of God shouted for joy.
The sky tells everyone about God's glory;
the vastness of the universe shows
that God has been at work.
Day after day it tells us this;
night by night this truth is revealed;
although not a sound is uttered,
the stars speak this message to everyone;
their story travels all over the world;
it is understood in lands far away.
When I survey the sky, your handiwork, dear God,
the moon and the stars which you set in their place,
I ask myself, what are mere human beings,
that you should pay us any attention?
Yet you have made us only slightly less than divine,
and crowned us with glory and honour.

Psalm 33:6; Genesis 1:16; Job 38:6–7; Psalms 19:1–4; 8:3–5

B LESSED are you, Lord, who made the two lights, sun and moon, and the stars for lights, for signs, for seasons, spring, summer, autumn, winter, days, weeks, months, years, to rule over day and night. Glory to you, Lord, for you created not only the visible light, but the light invisible, that which may be known of God, the law written in the heart.

Lancelot Andrewes

J ESUS was born in Bethlehem in the province of Judah when Herod was King. Suddenly some oriental astrologers turned up in Jerusalem. 'Where is the newborn King of the Jews?' they asked. 'We saw that his star was in the ascendant, and we have come to kneel before him.' . . .

There in front of them was the star which they had seen in the ascendant, and it moved until it stood over the place where the child was living. When the astrologers saw the star they were very happy; and when they came into the house they saw the child with Mary his mother. Throwing themselves down on their knees in front of him, they opened their valuables and made him a present of gold, frankincense and myrrh.

Matthew 2:1–2, 9–11

O God, who by a star guided the wise men to the worship of your Son; we pray you to lead to your-self the wise and the great of every land, that to you every knee may bow, and every thought be brought into cap-tivity, through Jesus Christ our Lord.

From the Church in Jerusalem and the Middle East

O God, by the study of the night sky
the wise men were led to your manger throne;
teach us to wonder at the beauty of your creation,
that we may be led on our way by the truth you reveal,
through Jesus Christ our Lord. Amen.

Michael Counsell

QUESTION the beautiful earth; question the beautiful sea; question the beautiful air, spread thinly over all the earth; question the beautiful heavens; question the arrangement of the constellations; question the sun brightening the day with its shining; question the moon, lessening with its splendour the darkness of the following night; question the living creatures that move about in the water, those that stay on land, and those that flit through the air – question all these things and they will all answer: 'Look and see! We are beautiful.' Their beauty is the sign of their agreement, that nobody could have made these beautiful transitory things, except the unchanging Beauty.

Augustine of Hippo

GOD showed me a tiny thing, no bigger than a hazel-nut, in the palm of my hand; it was as round as a ball. I looked at it and tried to understand; 'What is it?' I wondered. The answer I received was this: 'It is the whole created universe.' I was amazed that it had lasted so long, for it seemed to me as though it could suddenly have collapsed and disappeared, it was so small. Then I was made to understand this: 'It has lasted until now, and it will last forever, only because God loves it.' And so every-thing there is, exists simply because of the love of God.

Julian of Norwich

YOU never enjoy the world aright, till you see how a grain of sand exhibiteth the wisdom and power of God. . . . You never enjoy the world aright, till the sea itself floweth in your veins, till you are clothed with the heavens, and crowned with the stars: and perceive yourself to be the sole heir of the whole world: and more than so, because men are in it who are everyone sole heirs, as well as you. Till you can sing and rejoice and delight in God as misers do in gold, and kings in sceptres, you will never enjoy the world.

Thomas Traherne

HOW sweet the moonlight sleeps upon this bank!
    Here will we sit, and let the sounds of music
Creep in our ears: soft stillness and the night
Become the touches of sweet harmony:
Sit, Jessica; look how the floor of heaven
Is thick inlaid with patines of bright gold.
There's not the smallest orb which thou behold'st
But in his motion like an angel sings,
Still choiring to the young-eyed cherubims;
Such harmony is in immortal souls;
But whilst this muddy vesture of decay
Doth grossly close it in, we cannot hear it.

William Shakespeare

THE spacious firmament on high,
    With all the blue ethereal sky,
And spangled heav'ns, a shining frame,
Their great original proclaim:
Th'unwearied sun, from day to day,
Does his creator's power display,
And publishes to every land
The work of an almighty hand.

Soon as the evening shades prevail,
The moon takes up the wondrous tale,
And nightly to the listening earth
Repeats the story of her birth:
Whilst all the stars that round her burn,
And all the planets, in their turn,
Confirm the tidings as they roll,
And spread the truth from pole to pole.

What though, in solemn silence, all
Move round the dark terrestrial ball?
What though nor real voice nor sound
Amid their radiant orbs be found?
In reason's ear they all rejoice,
And utter forth a glorious voice,
For ever singing, as they shine,
'The hand that made us is divine.'

Joseph Addison

The Starlight Night

LOOK at the stars! look, look up at the skies!
  O look at all the fire-folk sitting in the air!
The bright boroughs, the circle-citadels there!
Down in dim woods the diamond delves! the elves'-eyes!
The grey lawns cold where gold, where quickgold lies!
Wind-beat whitebeam! airy abeles set on a flare!
Flake-doves sent floating forth at a farmyard scare! –
Ah well! it is all a purchase, all is a prize.
Buy then! bid then! – What? – Prayer, patience, alms,
  vows.
Look, look: a May-mess, like on orchard boughs!
Look! March-bloom, like on mealed-with-yellow sallows!
These are indeed the barn; withindoors house

The shocks. This piece-bright paling shuts the spouse
Christ home, Christ and his mother and all his hallows.

Gerard Manley Hopkins

THE duteous day now closeth,
　　Each flower and tree reposeth,
Shade creeps o'er wild and wood:
Let us, as night is falling,
On God our Maker calling,
Give thanks to him, the Giver good.

Now all the heavenly splendour
Breaks forth in starlight tender
From myriad worlds unknown;
And man, the marvel seeing,
Forgets his selfish being,
For joy of beauty not his own.

His care he drowneth yonder,
Lost in the abyss of wonder;
To heaven his soul doth steal:
This life he disesteemeth,
The day it is that dreameth,
That doth from truth his vision seal.

Awhile his mortal blindness
May miss God's lovingkindness,
And grope in faithless strife:
But when life's day is over
Shall death's fair night discover
The fields of everlasting life.

Paulus Gerhardt

To Night and Death

MYSTERIOUS Night! when our first parent knew
    Thee from report divine, and heard thy name,
Did he not tremble for this lovely frame,
This glorious canopy of light and blue?
Yet 'neath a curtain of translucent dew,
Bathed in the rays of the great setting flame,
Hesperus with the host of heaven came,
And lo! Creation widened in man's view.
Who could have thought such darkness lay concealed
Within thy beams, O Sun, or who could find,
Whilst fly and leaf and insect stood revealed,
That to such countless orbs thou mad'st us blind?
Why do we then shun Death with anxious strife?
If Light can thus deceive, wherefore not Life?

Joseph Blanco White

O Lord, while I am asleep,
    my heart will still be awake and worshipping you;
Permeate my sleep by your presence,
while the whole creation keeps watch over me,
singing with the angels,
and catching up my soul in its song of praise.

Gregory of Nazianzus

Dreams

Some see dreams as a projection of our own subconscious, but others regard them as another way in which God gives us his guidance or warning.

GOD has many ways of speaking to people,
and often they do not even notice.
In a dream or a vision during the night,
when people fall into a deep sleep,
while they slumber on their bed,
then God makes them hear instruction and understand it,
so that they turn back from their wicked deeds,
and are protected from the perils of pride.
Thus God saves us from destruction,
and draws us away from violent death.

Job 33:14–18

AT Gibeon, the Lord appeared to Solomon in a dream during the night, and asked him, 'What do you want me to give you?'

Solomon replied, '. . . Please give me, your servant, a wise mind to lead your people, and to decide between good and bad policies.'

1 Kings 3:5, 9

THE birth of Jesus the Messiah happened like this: his mother Mary was engaged to Joseph, but they did not yet live together. She was found to be pregnant, by means of the Holy Spirit. Her husband Joseph was a good man. He had no wish for her to be publicly disgraced, so he planned to have the engagement called off quietly. He had just made up his mind to do this, when an angel of the Lord appeared to him in a dream and said, 'Joseph, you are descended from King David. Do not be afraid to take Mary as your wife, for the baby she is expecting is from the Holy Spirit. She will have a baby boy, and you are to name him Jesus, which means "God saves", because he will save his people from their sins.' All this took place to fulfil what had been spoken by the Lord through the prophet: 'Look, the virgin will conceive and bear a son, and they shall name him Emmanuel,' which means, 'God is with us.' When Joseph woke up, he did what the angel of the Lord had told him to; he married Mary, but they did not sleep together until her baby boy was born; and Joseph named him Jesus.

Matthew 1:18–25

WHEN the astrologers came into the house, they saw the child with Mary his mother. Throwing themselves down on their knees in front of him, they opened their valuables and made him a present of gold, frankincense and myrrh. They had earlier had a dream in which they were warned not to go back to Herod, so they went back to their own country by a different route.

When they had gone, an angel of the Lord appeared to Joseph in a dream. 'Get up,' said the angel, 'take the child and his mother with you, and escape to Egypt. Stay there till I tell you that you can come back. Any day now King Herod will start looking for the child; he wants to kill him.' That night Joseph got up, took the child and his mother, and went to Egypt. They stayed there until King Herod died. . . .

When Herod died, at once an angel of the Lord appeared in a dream to Joseph in Egypt. 'Get up,' said the

angel. 'Take the child and his mother and go to the land of
Israel. The men who wanted to kill the child are dead.'

Matthew 2:11–14, 19–23

O God,
 you give the day for work and the night for sleep;
refresh our bodies and our minds
through the quiet hours of the night,
so that we may turn the eyes of our souls towards you,
and dream of your eternal glory. Amen.

The Leonine Sacramentary

Guiding and guarding

Sleeping or waking, we need God's guidance.

THE Lord is just and good,
 so he teaches sinners the way to live;
in his justice he guides humble people,
he teaches the humble his way.

Psalm 25:8–9

YET all the time you are with me;
 you take hold of my right hand;
you guide me with your wise advice,
and afterwards you will welcome me in glory.

Psalm 73:23–24

THE Lord will always guide you,
 in dry places he will satisfy your thirsty soul;
you will be like a well-watered garden,
like a spring that never dries up.

Isaiah 58:11

THE dawn light from above will rise on us,
shining on all who sit in death's dark shadow,
to guide our steps into the paths of peace.

Luke 1:79

GUIDE us, O Lord, waking,
and guard us sleeping,
that awake we may watch with Christ,
and asleep we may rest in peace.

The Breviary

ABIDE with us, O good Lord, through the night,
guarding, keeping, guiding, sustaining, sanctifying,
and with thy love gladdening us,
that in thee we may ever live,
and in thee may die;
through Jesus Christ our Lord. Amen.

Edward White Benson

O God,
from whom to be turned is to fall,
to whom to be turned is to rise,
and in whom to stand is to abide for ever:
grant us in all our duties your help,
in all our perplexities your guidance,
in all our dangers your protection,
and in all our sorrows your peace,
through Jesus Christ our Lord. Amen.

Augustine of Hippo

AS the compass-needle's arms
   point to North, South, East and West,
so the cross, through life's alarms,
helps us choose the way that's best.
Thank you, Lord, that you provide
this clear compass-cross to guide.

Where life's meaning is obscure,
through the valley of deep shade,
eyes are blind and hearts unsure;
Christ, our Sun, shine through to aid,
showing where before us lies
journey's end in paradise.

Transitory earthly things
break like bubbles in the breeze,
hopes dry up like desert springs,
plans may crash like rootless trees.
Drench dry land, O Lord, with rain,
till we bear the harvest grain.

Countless voices seek to guide,
many paths there are to choose,
if we turn to either side
firm ground soon our feet will lose.
Take us by the hand, we pray,
lead us on the narrow way.

Lord, through dusty ways ahead,
save the stumbling, here below,
be on every path we tread,
show lost sheep which way to go.
Guide us through the sheepfold's door,
till we come to joy once more.

Yang Yin-liu

O Lord, take our minds and think through them;
take our lips and speak through them;
take our lives and live out thy life;
take our hearts and set them on fire with love for thee;
and guide us ever by thy Holy Spirit,
through Jesus Christ our Lord. Amen.

William H. M. H. Aitken

THE night is here.
Dearest Jesus, still be near,
Like a candle in my heart,
Till sin's shadows all depart.

Soon will be morn.
Dearest Jesus, bring the dawn,
When the sun of righteousness
Shines in strength to warm and bless.

The moon shines bright.
Dearest Jesus, may your light
Shine to guide me evermore,
Till I come to heaven's door.

The starlight gleams.
Dearest Jesus, by your beams
Show the truth so crystal clear,
That your glory may appear.

Johann Freylinghausen

Wrestling with God

Our dreams may reflect the struggles of our daily life, including wrestling to know God in prayer.

THAT night, when Jacob was left alone, someone wrestled with him until the break of day. Then the person said, 'Let me go, for the day is dawning.'

But Jacob replied, 'I won't let you go, unless you give me your blessing.'

So the person said to him, 'What is your name?'

He answered, 'Jacob.'

Then the person said, 'You shall not be called Jacob any more; your name will be Israel, which means "Struggling with God"; for you have struggled with both the divine and the human, and you won!'

Then Jacob asked, 'Please tell me your name.'

But he replied, 'Why do you ask my name?' There and then he blessed him.

So Jacob called the place Peniel, which means 'Seeing God', for he said, 'I have seen God face to face, and yet I am still alive!'

Genesis 32:24–30

Wrestling Jacob

COME, O thou traveller unknown,
  Whom still I hold, but cannot see,
My company before is gone,
And I alone am left with thee;
With thee all night I mean to stay
And wrestle till the break of day.

I need not tell thee who I am,
My misery or sin declare;
Thyself hast called me by my name;
Look on thy hands, and read it there!
But who, I ask thee, who art thou?
Tell me thy name, and tell me now.

In vain thou strugglest to get free,
I never will unloose my hold;
Art thou the man who died for me?
The secret of thy love unfold.
Wrestling, I will not let thee go
Till I thy name, thy nature know.

Yield to me now, for I am weak,
But confident in self-despair;
Speak to my heart, in blessings speak,
Be conquered by my instant prayer!
Speak, or thou never hence shalt move, –
And tell me, if thy name is Love?

'Tis Love! 'tis Love! Thou diedst for me!
I hear thy whisper in my heart!
The morning breaks, the shadows flee;
Pure universal Love thou art!
To me, to all, thy bowels move;
Thy nature and thy name is Love!

My prayer hath power with God; the grace
Unspeakable I now receive;
Through faith I see thee face to face,
I see thee face to face, and live:
In vain I have not wept and strove;
Thy nature and thy name is Love.

Charles Wesley

Approaching Dawn

As the night wears on, we are encouraged by the appearance of the first light of dawn – a reminder that the night of death will be followed by a new and bright eternity.

L ORD, listen to my words and hear my sighs;
   Listen to my cry for help, my King and my God,
for it is to you that I pray.
Lord, in the morning you hear my voice;
in the morning I plead my case to you,
and then I wait for your answer.

Psalm 5:1–3

W AKE up, my soul!
      Wake up, my harp and lyre!
I myself will wake up the sun.
I will thank you, Lord, among all the nations,
your praise will be heard in every land.
For your love is higher than the heavens,
your faithfulness is vaster than the sky.

Psalm 108:1–4

I am waiting eagerly for the Lord,
   I trust him to keep his promise;
my soul waits for the Lord
more eagerly than sentries who watch for the day –
more eagerly than sentries who watch for the day.

Psalm 130:5–6

BEFORE the day dawns I cry for help;
   I have hope because of your promises.
I wake up before the sentries,
to meditate on your words.

Psalm 119:147–148

THE path that good people travel
   is like the first light of dawn,
which shines out brighter and brighter
until the full light of day.

Proverbs 4:18

THE roseate hues of early dawn,
   The brightness of the day,
The crimson of the sunset sky,
How fast they fade away!
O for the pearly gates of heaven,
O for the golden floor;
O for the Sun of righteousness
That setteth nevermore!

Mrs Cecil Frances Alexander

SAY not the struggle naught availeth,
   The labour and the wounds are vain,
The enemy faints not, nor faileth,
And as things have been they remain.

If hopes were dupes, fears may be liars;
It may be, in yon smoke conceal'd,
Your comrades chase e'en now the fliers,
And, but for you, possess the field.

For while the tired waves, vainly breaking,
Seem here no painful inch to gain,
Far back, through creeks and inlets making,
Comes silent, flooding in, the main.

And not by eastern windows only,
When daylight comes, comes in the light;
In front the sun climbs slow, how slowly!
But westward, look, the land is bright!

Arthur Hugh Clough

Ready for God's coming

Scripture often compares the need for us to be ready for the coming of Christ, in whatever way he comes to us, to watchers waiting for the dawn.

THINK of ways of encouraging each other
to be kind and loving.
Don't give up the habit of meeting together,
as some people have done;
rather, you should give each other fresh enthusiasm,
especially now that you can see the Day approaching.

Hebrews 10:24–25

DEAR friends, you are not groping in the dark, to be
surprised by the Day like thieves shown up by the
dawn; no, you are all people who belong in the light of
day; we are not people of night and darkness.

1 Thessalonians 5:5

YOU know what time it is: now it is time to wake up! The time that God has fixed for rescuing us is nearer to us now than it was when we first became believers; the night is nearly over, the Day will soon dawn. Like soldiers at dawn, let us strip off the things people do in the dark, and take up the weapons we need to fight in the daylight. Let us live in such a way that we are not ashamed to be seen in the full light of day.

Romans 13:11–13

JESUS said, 'Watch out! Your minds must not be dulled by feasting and drinking, and all the worries of this life, or that Day might catch you unawares like a trap. For it will come to everyone everywhere on earth. Be on your guard! Keep praying for the strength to survive all these things that are going to happen, and to stand up bravely in front of the Son of Man.'

Luke 21:34–36

WAKE, awake, for night is flying,
      The watchmen on the heights are crying;
Awake, Jerusalem, at last!
Midnight hears the welcome voices,
And at the thrilling cry rejoices:
Come forth, ye virgins, night is past!
The Bridegroom comes, awake,
Your lamps with gladness take;
      Hallelujah!
And for his marriage-feast prepare,
For ye must go to meet him there.

Zion hears the watchmen singing,
And all her heart with joy is springing,
She wakes, she rises from her gloom;
For her Lord comes down all-glorious,
The strong in grace, in truth victorious,
Her Star is risen, her Light is come!
Ah come, thou blessed Lord,
O Jesus, Son of God,
    Hallelujah!
We follow till the halls we see
Where thou hast bid us sup with thee.

Now let all the heavens adore thee,
And men and angels sing before thee
With harp and cymbal's clearest tone;
Of one pearl each shining portal,
Where we are with the choir immortal
Of angels round thy dazzling throne;
Nor eye hath seen, nor ear
Hath yet attain'd to hear
    What there is ours,
But we rejoice, and sing to thee
Our hymn of joy eternally.

                                    Philipp Nicolai

M AKE us watchful and careful, O Lord, we pray, in
       waiting for the coming of your Son, Christ our
Lord; that when he does come and knock he may find us
not sleeping in sin, but awake; and rejoicing in his praises;
through the same Jesus Christ our Lord. Amen.

                                    The Gelasian Sacramentary

O Lord God,
   the life of mortals,
the light of the faithful,
the strength of those who labour
and the repose of the dead;
grant us a tranquil night
free from all disturbance;
that after an interval of quiet sleep,
we may, by your bounty,
at the return of light
be endued with activity from the Holy Spirit,
and enabled in security to render thanks to you;
   through Jesus Christ our Lord. Amen.

The Mozarabic Sacramentary

WE are like lamps, O God, waiting to be lit by the
   flame of your Holy Spirit; grant that we may be
filled with your holy gifts, and shine as blazing lights
before the presence of your Son at his coming. We make
our prayers in his name, Jesus Christ our Lord. Amen.

The Gelasian Sacramentary

MY God, I am thine;
   What a comfort divine,
What a blessing to know that my Jesus is mine!
In the heavenly Lamb
Thrice happy I am,
And my heart it doth dance at the sound of his name.

True pleasures abound
In the rapturous sound;
And whoever hath found it hath paradise found.
My Jesus to know,
And feel his blood flow,
'Tis life everlasting, 'tis heaven below!

Yet onward I haste
To the heavenly feast;
That, that is the fullness, but this is the taste;
And this I shall prove,
Till with joy I remove
To the heaven of heavens in Jesus's love.

Charles Wesley

Resurrection

The rising of the sun at dawn is a parable of our hope of rising to the new life of heaven after we sleep in death.

YOU will show me the path that leads to life;
because of your presence with me I am full of joy;
my pleasure is to be near you for ever and ever.

Psalm 16:11

I cried to you, Lord my God, and you healed me;
you brought me back from the brink of death;
you took me from the place of the dead and gave me life.

Psalm 30:3

WHEN the sabbath day was finished, Mary Magdalene, Mary the mother of James, and Salome bought spices to take with them for anointing the body of Jesus. Very early on Sunday morning, at sunrise, they went to the tomb. On the way they asked one another, 'Who is going to roll away the stone for us which is blocking the entrance to the tomb?' (It was a very large stone.)

Then they looked up, and saw that the stone had

already been rolled back. They went into the tomb, where they saw a young man, dressed in a white robe, sitting on the right side. This made them very frightened.

But the young man said to them, 'There's no need to be frightened. You are looking for Jesus of Nazareth, who was crucified. But he has been raised; he is not here. Look, there is the place they laid him. Now go and tell his disciples, and especially Peter, that he is going ahead of you to Galilee. If you go there, you will see him, just as he told you.'

Mark 16:1–7

JESUS Christ has been raised out of death. He is the beginning of the harvest, the first to wake up of those who by dying have fallen asleep. The Scriptures say it was because one man, Adam, disobeyed God, that death came into the world. So it is fitting that through one man, Jesus, the resurrection of the dead should begin. For as we all die because of our common humanity as descendants of Adam, we shall all come alive again because of our common Christianity, as believers in Jesus.

1 Corinthians 15:20–22

DEATH is nothing at all. . . . I have only slipped away into the next room. . . . I am I and you are you . . . whatever we were to each other that we are still. Call me by my old familiar name, speak to me in the easy way which you always used. Put no difference into your tone; wear no forced air of solemnity or sorrow. Laugh as we always laughed at the little jokes we enjoyed together. Play, smile, think of me, pray for me. Let my name be ever the household word that it always was. Let it be spoken without effect, without the ghost of a shadow on it. Life means all that it ever meant. It is the same as it ever was;

there is absolutely unbroken continuity. What is this death but a negligible accident? Why should I be out of mind because I am out of sight? I am but waiting for you, for an interval, somewhere very near just around the corner. . . . All is well.

Henry Scott Holland

AFTER this it was noised abroad that Mr Valiant-for-truth was taken with a summons, and had this for a token that the summons was true, that his pitcher was broken at the fountain. When he understood it, he called for his friends, and told them of it. Then said he, 'I am going to my fathers, and though with great difficulty I am got hither, yet now I do not repent me of all the trouble I have been at to arrive where I am. My sword I give to him that shall succeed me in my pilgrimage, and my courage and skill, to him that can get it. My marks and scars I carry with me, to be a witness for me, that I have fought his battles who now will be my rewarder.' When the day that he must go hence was come, many accompanied him to the river side, into which as he went, he said, 'Death, where is thy sting?' And as he went down deeper he said, 'Grave, where is thy victory?' So he passed over, and all the trumpets sounded for him on the other side.

John Bunyan

Crossing the Bar

SUNSET and evening star,
And one clear call for me!
And may there be no moaning of the bar,
When I put out to sea,

But such a tide as moving seems asleep,
Too full for sound and foam,
When that which drew from out the boundless deep
Turns again home.

Twilight and evening bell,
And after that the dark!
And may there be no sadness of farewell,
When I embark;

For though from out our bourne of time and place
The flood may bear me far,
I hope to see my Pilot face to face
When I have crossed the bar.

Alfred, Lord Tennyson

GOD, you have made the night shine
   with the brightness of the true light of Christ,
therefore, since we have known
   the wonder of that light on earth,
we pray that we may also perfectly enjoy it in heaven;
through Jesus Christ our Lord. Amen.

The Gelasian Sacramentary

WHAT is dying? I am standing on the sea shore.
   A ship sails to the morning breeze and starts for the
ocean. She is an object of beauty and I stand watching her
till at last she fades on the horizon, and someone at my
side says, 'She is gone.' Gone where? Gone from my sight,
that is all; she is just as large in the masts, hull and spars as
she was when I saw her, and just as able to bear her load
of living freight to its destination. The diminished size and
total loss of sight is in me, not in her; and just at the
moment when someone at my side says, 'She is gone,'

there are others who are watching her coming, and other voices take up a glad shout, 'There she comes' – and that is dying.

Charles Henry Brent

GRANT, O Lord,
that we may live in thy fear,
die in thy favour,
rest in thy peace,
rise in thy power,
reign in thy glory;
for the sake of thy Son,
Jesus Christ our Lord. Amen.

William Laud

FROM the unreal lead me to the real!
From darkness lead me to light!
From death lead me to immortality!

The Brihad-Aranyaka Upanishad

BRING us, O Lord God,
at our last awakening into the house and gate of
heaven,
to enter into that gate
and dwell in that house
where there shall be no darkness nor dazzling but one
equal light;
no noise nor silence but one equal music;
no fears nor hopes but one equal possession;
no ends nor beginnings but one equal eternity,
in the habitations of thy majesty and thy glory,
for ever and ever. Amen.

John Donne

O God of time and eternity, who makest us creatures of time, to the end that when time is over we may attain to thy blessed eternity; with time, which is thy gift, give us also wisdom to redeem the time lest our day of grace be lost, for the sake of Christ Jesus our Lord. Amen.

Christina Rossetti

As watchmen wait for the morning,
so do our souls long for you, O Christ.
Come with the dawning of the day,
and make yourself known to us in the breaking of bread;
for you are our God for ever and ever. Amen.

The Mozarabic Sacramentary

A New Day

As dawn breaks, we look forward to another day of opportunities to serve God.

THIS is the day that the Lord has made:
let us rejoice and be glad in it!

Psalm 118:24

THE sun rises:
the animals creep away to their dens,
but human beings stride out to work until evening.

Psalm 104:22–23

PRAISE to thee, Lord Jesus Christ,
for all the benefits thou hast won for me,
for all the pains and insults thou hast born for me.
Most merciful redeemer, friend and brother,
may I know thee more clearly,
love thee more dearly,
and follow thee more nearly,
day by day. Amen.

Richard of Chichester

DECK thyself, my soul, with gladness,
Leave the gloomy haunts of sadness,
Come into the daylight's splendour,
There with joy thy praises render
Unto him, whose boundless grace
Grants thee at his feast a place;
He whom all the heavens obey
Deigns to dwell in thee today.

Hasten as a bride to meet him,
And with loving reverence greet him,
Who with words of life immortal
Now is knocking at thy portal;
Haste to make for him a way,
Cast thee at his feet, and say:
Since, oh Lord, thou com'st to me,
Never will I turn from thee.

Johann Franck

GOD'S true love is surely not ended,
God's compassion has not ceased;
they are new every morning,
as sure as the sunrise.
The Lord is all I have;
so I will wait in patient hope.
The Lord is good to those who trust,
sending help to all who seek;
so it is best to wait patiently –
to wait patiently for the Lord to save us.

Lamentations 3:22–26

O God, the author of eternal light, shed forth continual day upon us who watch for you, that our lips may praise you, our lives may bless you, and our meditations on the morrow glorify you, through Jesus Christ our Lord. Amen.

The Sarum Missal

LORD, go with each of us to rest; if any awake, temper to them the dark hours of watching; and when the day returns, return to us, our sun and comforter, and call us up with morning faces and with morning hearts, eager to labour, eager to be happy, if happiness should be our portion, and if the day be marked for sorrow, strong to endure it.

Robert Louis Stevenson

O God, the God of all goodness and of all grace,
   who art worthy of a greater love
than we can either give or understand:
fill our hearts, we beseech thee, with such love toward
   thee
that nothing may seem too hard for us
to do or to suffer in obedience to thy will;
and grant that loving thee,
we may become daily more like thee,
and finally obtain the crown of life
which thou hast promised to those who love thee;
through Jesus Christ our Lord. Amen.

Brooke Foss Westcott

O Lord Jesus Christ,
   the Way, the Truth and the Life,
grant that we may never stray from you who are the Way,
nor distrust you who are the Truth,
nor rest in any thing other than you, who are the Life.
Teach us by your Holy Spirit what to believe,
what to do,
and wherein to take our rest.
For your own name's sake we ask it,
O Jesus Christ our Lord. Amen.

Desiderius Erasmus

WHEN shall these longings be sufficed
That stir my spirit night and day?
When shall I see my country lay
Her homage at the feet of Christ?

Of all I have, O Saviour sweet,
All gifts, all skill, all thoughts of mine,
A living garland I entwine,
And offer at thy lotus feet.

Narayam Vaman Tilak

LORD Jesus, acknowledge what is of you in us, and
take away from us all that is not of you; for your
honour and glory. Amen.

Bernardino of Siena

O Lord God,
perfect in us that which is lacking of thy gifts:
of faith, to increase it;
of hope, to stablish it;
of love, to kindle it;
and make us to fear but one thing only,
the fearing aught more than thee,
our Father, our Saviour, our Lord,
for ever and ever. Amen.

Lancelot Andrewes

DEAREST Lord, teach me to be generous;
teach me to serve you as you deserve;
to give and not to count the cost,
to fight and not to heed the wounds,
to toil and not to seek for rest,
to labour and not to ask for any reward,
save that of knowing that I do your will.

Ignatius Loyola

REMEMBER, O Lord, what thou hast wrought in us,
and not what we deserve;
and as thou hast called us to thy service,
make us worthy of our calling;
through Jesus Christ our Lord. Amen.

The Leonine Sacramentary

GRACIOUS and holy Father,
give us wisdom to perceive you,
intelligence to understand you,
diligence to seek you,
patience to wait for you,
eyes to behold you,
a heart to meditate on you,
and a life to proclaim you;
through the power of the Spirit
of Jesus Christ our Lord. Amen.

Benedict of Nursia

O God, you divide the day from the night;
separate our deeds from the darkness of sin,
that we may continually live in your light,
and reflect in all our deeds your eternal beauty. Amen.

The Leonine Sacramentary

LOOK to this day! For it is life, the very life of life.
In its brief course lie all the varieties and realities of
your existence: the bliss of growth, the glory of action, the
splendour of beauty. For yesterday is already a dream,
and tomorrow is only a vision, but today, well-lived,
makes every yesterday a dream of happiness, and every
tomorrow a vision of hope. Look well, therefore, to this
day! Such is the salutation of the dawn.

Sanskrit

IT is glory enough for me that I should be your servant.
It is grace enough for me that you should be my Lord.

Arabic prayer

EVERY day is a messenger of God.

Russian proverb

AWAKE, my soul, and with the sun
Thy daily stage of duty run;
Shake off dull sloth, and joyful rise
To pay thy morning sacrifice.

Redeem thy mis-spent time that's past,
Live this day as if 'twere thy last:
Improve thy talent with due care;
For the great Day thyself prepare.

Let all thy converse be sincere,
Thy conscience as the noon-day clear;
Think how all-seeing God thy ways
And all thy secret thoughts surveys.

By influence of the light Divine
Let thy own light in good works shine;
Reflect all heaven's propitious ways
In ardent love and cheerful praise.

Wake, and lift up thyself, my heart,
And with the angels bear thy part,
Who all night long unwearied sing
High praise to the eternal King.

Direct, control, suggest, this day
All I design, or do, or say;
That all my powers, with all their might,
In thy sole glory may unite.

Praise God, from whom all blessings flow,
Praise him, all creatures here below,
Praise him above, ye heavenly host,
Praise Father, Son, and Holy Ghost. Amen.

Thomas Ken

MAY the blessed sunlight shine upon you and warm your heart till it glows like a great peat fire, so that the stranger may come and warm himself at it, as well as the friend.

Traditional Irish blessing

Index of Sources and Acknowledgements

All quotations from the Bible have been translated by the Editor.

Index of Subjects